# ORGANIC LIFESTYLE MADE EASY

## HOW TO CREATE A CHEMICAL-FREE HOUSEHOLD ONE STEP AT A TIME

**by Angela Cummings**

Publisher:
Metal Tree Publishing, LLC
N56W26142 Richmond Road
Sussex, WI 53089

Editor: Danielle Anderson

ISBN-13: 978-1-7320397-1-1

**First Edition:**
March 2018

# TABLE OF CONTENTS

# Acknowledgements

A special heartfelt thanks to family and friends who believed in me and those that thought I was full of crap. You have each helped me in different ways, to write this book and you have reminded me of the many different perspectives that exist. I'm so grateful for our candid conversations and your love.

To Dr. Glenn Toth who understood what was truly happening and helped me turn my health around.

To the countless authors, speakers, scientists, doctors, and organizations that work tirelessly to educate people, such as myself, about the chemicals in our everyday products that are causing illnesses.

To the companies developing, manufacturing, and selling products that are *truly* healthier for people. To the business owners that create restaurants, grocery stores, coffee shops, and retail spaces with fewer chemicals. Without your commitment, leadership, and action to create the products and environments with fewer chemicals, my ability to write this book would have been hindered.

## Dedication

To my son for his patience, love, respect, understanding, and support through life's ups and downs with "stupid allergies" and the medical challenges over the years.

# Forward

In 2000, shortly after moving into our newly-purchased five-year-old home, my son and I developed chronic sinusitis. In common terms that means a sinus infection all. of. the. time. And by all of the time, I mean antibiotics prescribed 12 months a year for three weeks at a time.

We spent 88% of our time in a state of infection and nearly all of our time being sick. It was not a case of over-prescribed medication. CT scans showed the infection coming and going... and coming back again within days.

As an added bonus, the antibiotics (24/7, 274 days a year) caused a development of an allergy to antibiotics—all antibiotics sold at a pharmacy, except for one. My health was at a breaking point, and shortly, the only solution to a simple sinus infection would be to receive antibiotics via IV at the local hospital... a solution that would be expensive, inconvenient, and detrimental to our stable household to say the least.

After eight years, 11 doctors misdiagnosing the cause, and thousands upon thousands of dollars spent, I took control of our health. I paid attention to patterns of activity and illness and poured over our medical records charting instances of infection.

Eventually, I was able to determine that chemicals were causing our illnesses. With the help of doctor number 12, I was able to name and better understand what was happening with our health. Multiple Chemical Sensitivity (MCS). Unfortunately, MCS is becoming a more common-place and well-known illness.

This book is not about MCS or my personal journey, but rather to build awareness of the chemicals in everyday products that are affecting our health in many ways, and to utilize my experience and knowledge to help other people. I hope that the information I've gathered over the years, resources I turned to, and actions I take every day can be helpful to others looking to live a healthier life with fewer chemicals.

Many books about healthy living are focused on one piece of healthy living—food, home environment, or a specific type of illness. This book is meant to build awareness of the many sources of chemical exposure (in everyday products) and opportunities that we all have to feel better and live happier, healthier lives with fewer chemicals.

This book has tried-and-true practical tips and "do-able" actionable steps that can help you to lead a healthier life. Just as important, this book is not meant to be medical advice or diagnostic in nature.

The best way to take strategic steps towards living life with fewer chemicals is to start with actions that make the most impact in your life. Each chapter of this book will give you actions that you can incorporate into your life—one. step. at. a. time.

# Chapter 1
# Rip off the Bandage

Happiness. We all want it. We all search for it, over and over throughout our life journey. Sometimes we find it in a hot cup of coffee and conversation. Sometimes we find it in the "I love you" before bedtime. Sometimes in a special moment that makes us pause.

Wherever we find it, we prefer to feel good in that moment. Physically, socially, mentally feel good. In fact, we go to great lengths to feel good by eating healthier, exercising, practicing yoga and meditation, joining community and church groups, and entertaining friends and family in our decorated, updated homes.

We buy lotions and makeup that covers blemishes, dye our hair to make us look younger, fill closets with a style of clothing and shoes for every occasion, and spray fragrance to smell good when we're in public.

Here's the thing, though.

The very food, cosmetics, clothes, decorations, fragrances, and household products that we—that *you*—are buying may be costing you your happiness.

Ridiculous?

Not really.

There are chemicals in our everyday products that have been linked to short- and long-term illness. This is not my opinion that can be dismissed as "out there." It's the advice of experts based on evidence, as I have discovered.

Back in 2000, shortly after moving into our newly-purchased, five-year-old home, my son and I developed chronic sinusitis which is a constant sinus infection. We were a healthy family that caught a cold in the winter and had the typical throat-itching nose-dripping seasonal allergies that could be easily cleared up with allergy meds.

Within a few month of moving into our new house, our "allergies" got worse.

Much worse.

In common terms, chronic sinusitis means having a sinus infection all of the time.  And by all of the time, I mean we spent 88% of our time in a state of infection and 99% of our time being sick. Sinus scans showed the infections were coming and going, but doctors couldn't figure out why.

They chalked it up to "bad allergies." Until they couldn't ignore it any longer.

After eight years of nearly continuous antibiotics, I had become allergic to all but one prescription oral antibiotic. It was clear to me and my medical team that this pattern of chronic sinusitis could not continue.

Three medical doctors from three different health care organizations told me to "figure this out." They had no idea what the cause was.

I was angry and frustrated. And determined to figure it out.

I poured over four inches of medical records for days, analyzing the diagnosis of doctors and corresponding prescriptions that were filled at the local pharmacy. I'm not a doctor by any stretch of the imagination, and I didn't need to be in this case. By simply entering the data into a basic Excel spreadsheet, it hit me.

For a year and a half, my son and I were living in our home only 50% of the time, staying with a friend the remainder of the time to watch his children while he worked the third shift. The frequency of infections would rise and fall when we were living in and outside of our house. The pattern was clear as day.

As it turned out, it seemed that our new home was causing illness.

But that wasn't the only thing happening. The more I learned, the clearer it became that the chronic sinusitis seemed to be a symptom of a larger problem being caused by chemicals in building materials and everyday products—the same products that millions of people use every day.

Before we continue on, I want to give you a heads up that this topic can be overwhelming, and has been for many people. I was overwhelmed myself when I first learned this information.

But here's the thing, my friends. We are raised to persevere and power through. And the best way to start is to rip off the bandage and jump right in. Together.

## Chemicals in Everyday Products

There are over 100,000 chemicals being used in various everyday products such as food, clothing, furniture, building materials, personal care products, and household items. Just let that sink in for a minute. Over ONE HUNDRED THOUSAND.

If you think that your health is not affected by these chemicals, think again.

Of the 100,000 chemicals, thousandssss (plural) of them are known to be harmful to human health.

*"More than 100,000 chemicals are used by Americans, and about 1,000 new chemicals are introduced each year. These chemicals are found in everyday items, such as foods, personal products, packaging, prescription drugs, and household and lawn care products. While some chemicals can be harmful, not all contact with chemicals is dangerous to your health." – U.S. Department of Health and Human Services* [1]

I'd like to say that the effects of all 100,000 chemicals are known; someday, perhaps that will be the case, but certainly not today. To keep it real, we need to recognize that not all chemicals are created equal. Some chemicals are harmless to humans. However, thousands have been identified as harmful. For the purposes of this book, anytime I refer to

---

[1] Agency for Toxic Substance and Disease Registry (ATSDR), Division of Health Assessment and Consultation, "Chemicals, Cancer, and You," Accessed December 12, 2015: 1.
https://www.atsdr.cdc.gov/emes/public/docs/Chemicals,%20Cancer,%20and%20You%20FS.pdf

"chemicals," I'm referring to chemicals that can be harmful to people's health.

For example, the over 1,400 chemicals and chemical groups that are known or likely to cause cancer.[2]

## Where Chemicals are Found

Chemicals can be found in a number of places—in our homes, places of business, stores, and restaurants. The very places where you and I eat, sleep, relax, play, and work. To use the term "everywhere" is a bit overwhelming but a fair statement to make.

"WHAT THE....!?" spilled out of my mouth when I first learned this.

I'm gonna be brutally honest with you. It was overwhelming for me.

Shut-down flat out life-stopping overwhelming.

It was one of two times in life that I had been paralyzed by reality. The first was when my son's father left me to raise our three-month-old son by myself...100% by myself. The second was this instance.

My mind spun in circles for days trying to wrap my head around it all. Around the idea that chemicals were in nearly all of the products we were buying. Around the idea that they were causing serious illnesses. Around the idea that this was

---

[2] Curt DellaValle, "The Pollution in People: Cancer-Causing Chemicals in Americans' Bodies," EWG Original Research, June 14, 2016. https://www.ewg.org/research/pollution-people#.WIllyqinHIU

allowable and legal! Around the idea that I had to make a life change in order to live a healthier life.

I was mad, overwhelmed, and in shock. And so grateful to the experts that had been studying this topic and could help me to understand it better.

Scientists have found chemicals, the type that are harmful to our health, in many categories of products such as food, cleaners, personal care products, building materials, furniture, and household items. What's *in* them, *on* them, and *around* them is influencing our health.

What does that mean? What products am I exactly talking about? The two tables below are partial lists of products where chemicals have been found. These lists were compiled from data resources referenced in this book. It's not even a complete list; that could be an entire book in and of itself.

The intention of this partial list is to give you an understanding of the widespread use of chemicals in our everyday products.

# Table 1: List of Various Products that can Give off VOCs (chemicals harmful to peoples' health)

adhesive (glue) removers
adhesives
aerosol or liquid insect pest products
aerosol penetrating oils
aerosol spray products for some paints
air fresheners
antimicrobials
artificial flowers
automotive parts, tops floor mats
automotive products
blood and respiratory tubing
blood bags
brake cleaner

building materials
built-in and modular casework
car exhaust (attached garage)
carbonless copy paper
carburetor cleaner
carpet backing
carpet padding
carpeting

catheters
caulks
ceiling tiles
chemical solvents
citrus (orange) oil or pine oil
cleaning products
clothing/textiles

disinfecting products
door and window frames
downspouts

dry cleaned clothes

drywall
electrical insulation
electrical wiring
electronics
electronics cleaners

entrance floor mats
fabric/leather cleaners
fabrics
feeding tubes
fiberglass-sandwich-panel assemblies
finishes

flashing
flexible plastic
flooring
fluorescent lamps
foams
food "shrink wrapped" packages
food containers
food packaging
food plastic wrap
freezers
fuel oil
fuels
furniture (home)

coatings
colognes
compact disks
composite wood
construction activities
contact cement
containers
copy machines
correctional fluid
cosmetics
countertops
credit cards
curtains and drapes

degreasers
dehumidifiers
deodorizers
ink
insulation
intravenous (IV) bags
irrigation systems
juices
kerosene
laminate wood
laminated-Wood
leather treatments
lighting fixtures
mechanical systems
mineral spirits
model cement
mold inhibitors
molding
moth balls
moth flakes
nail care products

furniture (office)
furniture polishes
garden hoses
gasketing
gasoline
glues
gutters
hair spray
heart and bypass tubing
hobby supplies
hoses
HVAC systems
impact-resistant safety
equipment
infant and baby bottles
infant feeding cups
inflatable recreational toys
reusable cups
roof membranes
roofing
rubbing alcohol
sealant liners
sealants
shades and blinds
shoe soles
shower curtains
siding
solvents
spot removers
spray lubricants
stain repellant enhancers
stains
stored supplies
stored trash
stretched-fabric wall
systems (cubicles)

nail polish
nail polish remover
office equipment (printers and copiers)
packaging materials

paint stripper
paint thinner
paints (interior and exterior)
paper and textile finishes
parts of dialysis devices
perfumes
pest management methods
pesticides
pipes and conduit
plastic bags
plastic dinnerware
plastic furniture
plastic swimming pool
plumbing pipes
plywood
polishes
pressed-wood products
primer
PVC cement
rain coats
refrigerant from air conditioners
refrigerators

subfloor
swimming pool liners

switches
toilet, bath and laundry accessories
toys
under slab water barriers
upholstered furniture
upholstery and seat covers
upholstery fabric
varnishes and wax
vehicle exhaust
vertical Louver Blinds
videodiscs
vinyl flooring
vinyl siding
wall and corner guards
wall covering (wall paper)
wall protection
water bottles
water repellents
water resistance products
weather stripping
window (vinyl)
window treatments
wire and cable coatings

wood (decks, framing materials, doors, trim, paneling)

## Table 2: List of Personal Care Items and Cosmetics that may Contain Chemicals (harmful to health)

acne treatments
aftershave
anti-aging creams
antibacterial soaps
anti-itch creams
antiperspirant
baby bottles
baby lotions
baby powder
baby shampoos
baby soaps
baby washes
blush
body lotions
body washes
bubble bath
cellulite cream
cologne

colored shampoo
conditioner
cosmetic bottles
cosmetics
curl creams
dandruff shampoos
defrizzer
dental sealants
deodorant
dyes and synthetic colors
exfoliants

eye makeup

hair dye
hair gel
hair relaxers
hair spray
hair straighteners
hair-growing products
henna dyes
keratin hair treatments
lipstick
liquid powder
lotion
makeup
mascara
medical devices
medications
metalloestrogens
microwave oven dishes
moisturizers
most makeup or lip balms with SPF
mouse
mouthwashes
nail hardener
nail polish
nail strengthener
nail treatments
nipple cream
paneling
perfume
perms
psoriasis and dandruff shampoos

eye shadows
eyelash glue
face lotions
face powder
face wash
facial cleansers
foot scrubs
foundation
fragrances
furniture polish
hair bleach
hair colors

relaxers
scrubs
shampoo
skin care products
skin lighteners
soap body wash
soaps
sunscreen
toothpaste

Taking a few items from the list, let's apply it to real life and two scenarios that we can all relate to. Meal time and bed time.

What are we exposed to when preparing and eating dinner?

- Countertops that you prepare food on (named on the list as countertops)
- Plates and cups that you drink from (named on the list as plastic dinnerware)
- Kitchen table and chairs that you sit on (named on the list as furniture)
- Cleaners used to clean countertops, plates and cups, and the kitchen table (named on the list as cleaning products)
- Food and drink you are about to consume (named on the list as pesticides, food containers, and food packaging)

How about during bed time?

- Bed, sheets and blankets, and pajamas (named on the list as clothing/textiles)
- Night stands and dressers (named on the list as furniture and pressed wood products)
- Wall paint (named on the list as paints)

What are each of those products made of? What's on them? What's in them? How are they affecting our home environment and health?

Sleep is a time that our bodies recover, repair, and re-energize. But here's the thing. Hormone-altering chemicals are regularly found in beds, pajamas (clothing), sheets, and blankets. Night stands, dressers, and wall paints are letting off gases (called VOCs, which we'll get into later) that have been linked to chronic and terminal illnesses...right into your bedroom.

I'm not trying to be scary here. Applying knowledge is an important step in understanding how to solve the problem.

## Safe Levels
When experts state that a product has a safe level of a chemical, they are referring to that ONE product. Look around your house. How many products do you have? Let's take an easy-to-identify category of products—plastic.

Let's pretend that having 10 plastic products in your home is deemed "safe." Now count the number of plastic products in your home. Here's what our house with a family of two used to look like:

8 plastic dishes
8 plastic cups
20 plastic storage containers with lids
28 large plastic storage bins
4 vines of plastic decorative leafs
14 sheets of plastic holiday clings
5 plastic cooking utensils
2 large bins worth of plastic building blocks
20+ numerous plastic action heroes (10+), swords (4), hats (4), toy guns (2)
3 plastic soap dishes/liquid pump containers
5 garbage bags, garbage cans
6 picture frames
<u>3 blow dryers and flat irons</u>
126+ Total

Easily, we had over 120 items that were plastic. This doesn't take into account composite wood furniture (made partly of plastic), plastic piping, or building materials that are made with plastic.

If 10 pieces is deemed as safe, we exceeded the safe limit by more than 110 items—an excess of 92% for our little family of two.

And that's only one category of products with harmful chemicals in them.

There are hundreds (300, 400, 500) of products in each of our homes that can contain harmful chemicals. As a quick example, take the 120 items listed above and add to it the list of products below that took me five minutes to whip together.

Again, it's based on items bought for our family of two.

| | |
|---|---|
| Bed box springs | 2 |
| Bed mattresses | 2 |
| Bed mattress covers | 2 |
| Bed sheets | 2 |
| Bed blankets | 2 |
| Pillows | 2 |
| Night stands (two in my room) | 3 |
| Dressers | 2 |
| Couches (living room and family room) | 2 |
| Chairs  (living room and family room) | 2 |
| Drapes (14 windows, varying sizes) | 14 |
| Underwear | 14 |
| Bras | 7 |
| Shirts – short sleeve | 14 |
| Shirts – long sleeve | 14 |
| Sweatshirts/Sweaters | 14 |
| Shorts | 14 |
| Pants | 14 |
| Jackets  (spring/fall and winter) | 4 |
| Shoes & boots | 6 |
| TVs | 2 |
| Electronics (stereo, DVD player, game consoles, etc.) | 9 |
| Carpet (rooms) | 2 |
| Laminate wood (rooms) | 3 |
| Vinyl (rooms) | 3 |
| Shower curtain | 1 |
| Paint (fresh) | 9 |
| Composite wood picture frames | 12 |
| Soaps (dishwasher, hand, shampoo, etc.) | 5 |
| Cleaners | 6 |
| | 188 |

That's a total of 314 products, simply off the top of my head for a small family of two in a plain Jane middle class house. A family of four would have double the number of beds, clothing, pillows, etc. You can see how easily 3-4-500 products can accumulate.

If the products each contain a mid-level amount of chemicals, does that equate to a safe level of chemicals in your home? Plain logic and scientific indoor air quality testing will likely tell us it is not safe.

"The scientists of the Halifax Project identified 85 chemicals common in the environment that are capable of disrupting hallmark pathways in the body – and the search for these types of chemicals is just beginning. What is alarming is these chemicals are not only common in the environment, they are common in people as well."[3]

Before we look at how exactly these chemicals may be affecting health, let's look at what chemicals we're talking about.

**Need-to-Know Basis**
We've talked about where harmful chemicals can be found, but what exact chemicals are we talking about?

Now, I'm going to be upfront—I'm not going to list the specific chemical names and expect you to check every label of every product. This amount of information will drive you mad, not to mention the amount of time it would take.

---

[3] Curt DellaValle, "The Pollution in People: Cancer-Causing Chemicals in Americans' Bodies," EWG Original Research, June 14, 2016. https://www.ewg.org/research/pollution-people#.WIllyqinHIU

Most of us don't have the time to sort through the lists of thousands of chemicals anyway, and frankly, most of us don't want to. Having said that, it's always good to be informed, so if you *do* want to know the names of specific chemicals, check out these helpful resources:

- U.S. Department of Health and Human Services Agency for Toxic Substances and Disease Register (ATSDR) found at https://www.atsdr.cdc.gov/
- Environmental Working Group found at https://www.ewg.org/
- *A to Z of D-Toxing: The Ultimate Guide to Reducing Our Toxic Exposures*, by Sophia Ruan Gushee

While we won't go through specific chemical names, there are a few overarching facts that may be helpful for you to know.

1. No one, including the Environmental Protection Agency (EPA) and Food and Drug Administration (FDA), knows how the majority of the over 100,000 chemicals are affecting people's health. Beyond that, government regulations change with administrations and the level of rigor and definition of "safe products" is constantly changing. You and I can't rely solely on the government to keep us safe.

2. Chemicals are being produced at a pace that is far greater than the capacity for the government and third-party, privately-owned organizations to test and fully understand them. As the ole heckle goes, the government has red tape slowing it down. As a former government employee, I say this with love for my

fellow former colleagues. However, even privately-owned companies have a hard time keeping up with the pace of testing new chemicals for their affects on people's health.

It's not just limited to new chemicals, though. We have chemicals. And then we have chemicals combined together. When chemicals are combined together, they can have an entirely different toxic reaction. Think of what happens when bleach and ammonia are combined—it is a significantly more dangerous substance. Please don't try mixing them to find out.

3. Not only are there over 100,000 chemicals, but some have more than one name. Yeesh.

   Assume for a moment that there are only two alternate names for each of the 102 chemicals that have been linked to breast cancer.[4] Simple math says that 100 + 200 (100x2 alternate names) = 300 chemical names for you, as a consumer, to remember to search for in each product you purchase.

> *"Unfortunately, many of the substances and exposures on the list below can often go by different names. This can make it hard to find a particular substance on one or both of these lists, which are alphabetical order and may not always use the most common terms." — Known and Probable Human Carcinogens. 1.25.17. Cancer.org*

---

[4]Ruthann A. Rudel, et all, "New Exposure Biomarkers as Tools for Breast Cancer Epidemiology, Biomonitoring, and Prevention: A Systematic Approach Based on Animal Evidence," Environmental Health Perspectives. doi: 10.1289/ehp.1307455. https://ehp.niehs.nih.gov/1307455/

Even though breast cancer affects a large number of women in the United States, it is only one of many health issues that scientists have found that may be caused by the thousands of chemicals in our everyday products.

In short, it would take an insane amount of time to check every product you buy to make sure it didn't contain chemicals that may be harmful to human health.

Stated even shorter: Ugh. Nope. Not gonna happen.

4. While Europe has understood (and been vocal about) chemicals in everyday products that are causing health conditions, the USA is just starting to understand and accept this idea. In fact, there are specific products that have been sold in Europe with *non-toxic chemicals* but sold in the U.S. *with* toxic chemicals.

   Let that sink in for a moment.

   We'll discuss this more in Chapter 7 – Personal Care Products.

5. Studies can show conflicting information. Who do you and I, as consumers concerned about our health, listen to? The fact of the matter is that studies can say anything you want them to. Well, not what YOU want them to. They can say whatever the funder wants them to.

Some studies are paid for by the very company or industry that manufacturers the product. In that case, the manufacturer has a vested interest—something to gain from a positive study, namely a favorable increase in sales.

I've worked in the non-profit, government, and for-profit fields where entities received funding from a variety of sources. At the end of the day, if the funder was unhappy with performance or outcomes, the funding would, well, stop (legally and legitimately). Money talks.

Follow the money trail. That'll show you who the true customer is. Always follow the money trail.

The beauty of having a third-party independent review of products that is paid for by the consumers is that it allows the *consumers* to have the ultimate power.

Thank the heavens, universe, God, Buddha, or whatever higher power that you believe in (if you do) that there are companies that are testing products for people like me—like YOU—that don't have the time, patience, or mental capacity to check each and every product for chemicals that may be harming our health, the health of our family, and the health of our friends.

*"With a regulatory system offering little oversight into what goes into the products used in health care, institutions must look to the market to eliminate the "worst in class"*

*chemicals and to evaluate and encourage safer, healthier, and less toxic products." – Healthy Building Network[5]*

While not EVERY product and chemical has been tested and studied, there are several organizations working to provide unbiased, objective, and digestible information to consumers, empowering us—you and me—to make increasingly informed decisions every day. These organizations conduct research that is collectively paid by us, common consumers, to provide third-party independent review of products.

Organizations like the Environmental Working Group (www.ewg.org) are funded by consumer donations—money from you and me who have no vested interest except for the protection of our health. These organizations are necessary. They are working for us, looking out for our best interest.

They are methodically identifying which chemicals are damaging human cells in a way that can lead to illnesses ranging from "bad allergies" and obesity to cancer and organ failure.

So why didn't our doctors know about this? They did... but they dismissed it.

---

[5] Healthy Building Network, "Toxic Chemicals in Building Materials: An Overview for Health Care Organizations," Fact Sheet: Toxic Chemicals in Building Materials, May 2008: 1.
https://healthybuilding.net/uploads/files/toxic-chemicals-in-building-materials.pdf

# Chapter 2
# What's Happening to Our Health

When it came to identifying the cause of my (and my son's) chronic sinusitis, the three doctors that instructed me to "figure it out" dismissed my suggestions that our illness may be tied to chemicals in products that my son and I (and people in general) were exposed to everyday.

While the medical community had a few medical doctors such as Dr. William Rae and Dr. Grace Ziem that had studied and understood how chemicals in everyday products were affecting people's health, the doctors we had seen back in the early 2000s thought the idea was nonsense.

Ironic, I thought, that after emphasizing the importance of finding a resolution, spending thousands of dollars in medical bills for eight years, seeing more than 10 doctors from various health organizations that recognized a problem indeed existed but were stumped, no one was interested in what I had found.

Heartbreaking. Not only for me, but for others that were experiencing similar health problems with no resolution.

As I mentioned, over 140 medical conditions may be caused by chemicals in our everyday products—medical conditions that have rapidly increased in frequency over the years with no explanation as to why.

Fast forward to today. The Center for Disease Control, Harvard School of Public Health, U. S. Department of Health and Human Services and over 20 other health-focused organizations recognize the very idea that our doctors had waived away.

Chemicals in standard everyday products may be damaging the cells in our bodies and causing chronic and terminal health conditions.

**What's Happening?**
Our bodies *want* to take care of us. However, they can't when you and I are damaging our cells—the very cells that were meant to keep us healthy.

I'm gonna get a little nerdy here about cells.

As I've mentioned, chemicals may be damaging our bodies at a cellular level—this means the very cells that make up our skin, bones, muscles, organs, and brain.

Chemicals can damage cells in a number of ways: damage to the cell membrane that produces energy, the ribosomes which make proteins and enzymes, the DNA which affects genetics, membrane receptor sites which are responsible for hormones, and other cell messenger sites that our bodies need in order to communicate within that cell, with other cells, and with each of the body's organs.[6]

To be honest, I have no idea what a ribosome or membrane receptor site is. But I do know this—damage to our cells in any way cannot be good for anyone.

When cells are damaged, they create inflammation and free radicals. In turn, they cause an array of problems:

1. **Sensitization.** It sounds like nice soft sediment of "oh, shooty, I'm sensitive." In reality, it's an ugly hypersensitivity to one or many things. In my personal experience, my allergists (plural) diagnosed me with "bad allergies," when in fact it was not an allergy at all but a sensitivity that had developed due to chemical damage.

2. **Repeated damage to cells.** Damaged cells are inflamed and create free radicals that damage other cells. Those damaged cells become inflamed and create free radicals that damage other cells. This process repeats itself, having a snowball effect on the body.

   A second snowball effect occurs when detoxification is impaired. That creates more free radicals which impairs detoxification even more, which creates more

---

[6] "Neutral Sensitization: The Medical Key to Treatment of Chemical Injury (pg2)," Chemical Injury.net, Accessed February 7, 2017, http://www.chemicalinjury.net/html/neural_sensitization-pg_2.html

free radicals and more problems with detoxing. Snowball effect #2.[7]

"For everyone, minimizing this vicious cycle is vital to health," according to Dr. Grace Ziem. She goes on to say that all inflammatory and degenerative disease and cancer risk can be greatly reduced.[8]

3. **Damage to major organ cells.** Cellular damage impairs (limits) the function of brain cells, nerve cells, and heart cells.

4. **Impairment of all body functions.** This can include (but is not limited to) the following functions:[9]

| Body Function Affected | Effect on Body |
|---|---|
| Energy | Fatigue |
| Body Temperature | Lowered body temperature |
| Hormones | Impaired ability to produce and regulate hormones |
| Nutrients | Impaired ability to absorb nutrients |

---

[7] "How Chemical Injury/Chemical Sensitivity Affects the Body," Chemical Injury.net, Accessed February 7, 2017, http://chemicalinjury.net/html/how_chemical_injury_chemical_s.html

[8] "Long Term Treatment," (pg11) Chemical Injury.net, Accessed February 7, 2017, http://www.chemicalinjury.net/html/neural_sensitization-pg_11.html

[9] "How Chemical Injury/Chemical Sensitivity Affects the Body," Chemical Injury.net, Accessed February 7, 2017, http://chemicalinjury.net/html/how_chemical_injury_chemical_s.html

| Digestion | Impaired ability to generate enzymes and acid needed for digesting food |
| --- | --- |
| Repair & Maintenance | Impaired ability to make proteins to repair and maintain cells |
| New Cells | Impaired ability to generate new cells or replace aging or damaged cells |
| Bones | Impaired ability to maintain proper bone structure and density |
| Detoxification | Impaired ability to detoxify |
| Communication | Impaired ability for cells to send messages to other body cells |
| Nerves | Impaired ability for messages to pass within the brain and from the brain to the nerves |
| Blood & Oxygen | Impaired ability for blood to flow through blood vessels, reducing the supply of oxygen and nutrients to organs |

In addition, damaged cells can affect circulation,[10] the liver, kidneys, lungs/respiratory tract, and the endocrine and immune systems. It can accelerate degenerative diseases, increase osteoporosis of bones, and speed up the aging process.[11]

---

[10] "How Chemical Injury/Chemical Sensitivity Affects the Body," (pg 2) Chemical Injury.net, Accessed February 7, 2017, http://www.chemicalinjury.net/html/how_chemical_injury_chemical_s1.html
[11] "How Chemical Injury/Chemical Sensitivity Affects the Body," (pg 2) Chemical Injury.net, Accessed February 7, 2017, http://www.chemicalinjury.net/html/how_chemical_injury_chemical_s1.html

So... basically everything.

Stick with me here. Believe it or not, there are small, easy, achievable steps that will make a big impact. I've done it. Other people have done it. And you can do it too.

But first we have a little more science to get through.

Our bodies are made up of 100 trillion cells. Paaah! That's a lot. Individual cells are organized into tissues; different kinds of tissues form an organ. Each organ is a member of an organ system.[12]

Our bodies have 10 major organ systems, many of which can be affected by chemicals in our everyday products in ways that you may not think of.

The Center for Disease Control (CDC) Agency for Toxic Substances and Disease Registry (ATSDR) mentions a few of the possible effects in their publication, *Health Effects of Chemical Exposure*. Here's a quick synopsis of the possible effects from harmful chemicals found in everyday products and an overview of the organ systems:

Nervous System
"Possible health effects of the nervous system include inability to move, loss of feeling, confusion, and decreased speech, sight, memory, muscle strength, or coordination."[13]

---

[12] National Geographic, Human Body 101, Video, Accessed February 7, 2017, https://www.nationalgeographic.com/science/health-and-human-body/human-body/

[13] Agency for Toxic Substance and Disease Registry (ATSDR), Division of Health Assessment and Consultation, "Health Effects of Chemical Exposure," Accessed February 7, 2017: 3.

This organ system includes the brain, spinal cord, and nerves, and it's responsible for controlling body activity. "The nervous system is the major controlling, regulatory, and communicating system in the body. It is the center of all mental activity including thought, learning, and memory."[14] "The brain sends messages through the spinal cord and nerves of the peripheral nervous system to control the movement of the muscles and the function of internal organs."[15]

Endocrine System
"Exposure to these chemicals can play tricks on our bodies by increasing the production of certain hormones while decreasing the production of others, which can lead to lower IQs and behavioral problems in children, endometriosis in adult women, and diabetes and infertility."[16]

This organ system includes glands such as pancreas, pituitary, thyroid, and adrenal, and it's responsible for

---

https://www.atsdr.cdc.gov/emes/public/docs/Health%20Effects%20of%20Che mical%20Exposure%20FS.pdf

[14] "Introduction to the Nervous System," SEER Training Module, National Institute of Health, National Cancer Institute, Accessed February 22, 2017. https://training.seer.cancer.gov/anatomy/nervous/

[15] "What are the parts of the nervous system?," Health research throughout the lifespan, National Institute of Health, Eunice Kennedy Shriver National Institute of Child Health and Human Development, Accessed February 27, 2017. https://www.nichd.nih.gov/health/topics/neuro/conditioninfo/parts

[16] Alex Formuzis and Violet Batcha, "IQs Plummet and Healthcare Costs Surge From Endocrine Disrupting Chemicals," EWG News and Analysis, October 20, 2016. https://www.ewg.org/enviroblog/2016/10/iqs-plummet-and-healthcare-costs-surge-endocrine-disrupting-chemicals#.WlldJKinHIU

generating hormones that regulate growth, development, metabolic activities (metabolism), and more.[17]

## Cardiovascular System

"Possible health effects include heart failure and the inability of blood to carry the necessary oxygen to the body."[18]

This organ system includes the heart, arteries, veins, and capillaries (small blood vessels), and it's responsible for making sure that blood reaches every single part of the body—head to toes, skin to internal organs.

## Immune and Lymphatic Systems

"Possible health effects of the immune system include overreaction to environmental substances (allergy), immune system slow down or failure, and autoimmunity (autoimmunity causes the body to attack itself—which makes it more likely to have an over-reaction or infection)."[19]

This organ system includes the spleen, bone marrow, and lymph nodes (commonly referred to as "glands" even though they are actually lymph nodes).[20] It's responsible for the

---

[17] "Introduction to the Endocrine," SEER Training Module, National Institute of Health, National Cancer Institute, Accessed February 22, 2017.
https://training.seer.cancer.gov/anatomy/endocrine/

[18] Agency for Toxic Substance and Disease Registry (ATSDR), Division of Health Assessment and Consultation, "Health Effects of Chemical Exposure," Accessed February 7, 2017: 2.
https://www.atsdr.cdc.gov/emes/public/docs/Health%20Effects%20of%20Chemical%20Exposure%20FS.pdf

[19] Agency for Toxic Substance and Disease Registry (ATSDR), Division of Health Assessment and Consultation, "Health Effects of Chemical Exposure," Accessed February 7, 2017: 3.
https://www.atsdr.cdc.gov/emes/public/docs/Health%20Effects%20of%20Chemical%20Exposure%20FS.pdf

[20] "Your Immune System," Kids Health, Date Reviewed: May 2015.

immune system, which fights to keep our bodies healthy. The immune system, which includes the lymphatic system, has three primary functions: protect the body by fighting against microorganisms and disease (the bad guys), absorb fats and fat-soluble vitamins, and return extra tissue fluid to the blood.[21]

Respiratory System
"Possible health effects of the respiratory system include asbestosis, lung cancer, chronic bronchitis, fibrosis, emphysema, and decreased oxygen supply in blood."[22]

This organ system includes the lungs and breathing function. It's responsible for working with the circulatory system to provide oxygen and remove waste products of metabolism (e.g., carbon dioxide, etc.), and regulates pH of the blood.[23] The respiratory and circulatory systems provide our bodies energy 24 hours per day (the two systems include beating heart and lungs).[24]

---

http://kidshealth.org/en/kids/immune.html?ref=search#.

[21] "Introduction to the Lymphatic System," SEER Training Module, National Institute of Health, National Cancer Institute, Accessed February 22, 2017. https://training.seer.cancer.gov/anatomy/lymphatic/

[22] Agency for Toxic Substance and Disease Registry (ATSDR), Division of Health Assessment and Consultation, "Health Effects of Chemical Exposure," Accessed February 7, 2017: 2. https://www.atsdr.cdc.gov/emes/public/docs/Health%20Effects%20of%20Chemical%20Exposure%20FS.pdf

[23] "Introduction to the Respiratory System," SEER Training Module, National Institute of Health, National Cancer Institute, Accessed February 22, 2017. https://training.seer.cancer.gov/anatomy/respiratory/

[24] National Geographic, Human Body 101, Video, Accessed February 7, 2017, https://www.nationalgeographic.com/science/health-and-human-body/human-body/

## Digestive System

"Possible health effects of the hepatic system include liver damage, tumors, accumulation of fat (steatosis), and death of liver cells."[25]

This organ system includes the digestive tract, liver, gallbladder, pancreas, salivary glands, mouth, throat, stomach, and intestines. Tongue and teeth are accessories to the digestive system. It's responsible for turning food into liquefied food (breaks down food) and into energy.[26]

## Urinary System

"Possible health effects of the renal system include decreased formation of urine, decreased blood flow to kidney, decreased ability to filter the blood, prevented urine flow, kidney tissue damage, and kidney cancer."[27]

This organ system includes the kidneys and bladder, and it's responsible for removing liquid waste. "The major task of excretion still belongs to the urinary system. If it fails the

[25] Agency for Toxic Substance and Disease Registry (ATSDR), Division of Health Assessment and Consultation, "Health Effects of Chemical Exposure," Accessed February 7, 2017: 3.
https://www.atsdr.cdc.gov/emes/public/docs/Health%20Effects%20of%20Chemical%20Exposure%20FS.pdf

[26] National Geographic, Human Body 101, Video, Accessed February 7, 2017, https://www.nationalgeographic.com/science/health-and-human-body/human-body/

[27] Agency for Toxic Substance and Disease Registry (ATSDR), Division of Health Assessment and Consultation, "Health Effects of Chemical Exposure," Accessed February 7, 2017: 2.
https://www.atsdr.cdc.gov/emes/public/docs/Health%20Effects%20of%20Chemical%20Exposure%20FS.pdf.

other organs cannot take over and compensate adequately."[28]

## Reproductive System

"Possible health effects of the reproductive system include decreased ability to have a baby, increased baby deaths, increased birth defects, and infertility (the inability to have children)." [29]

This organ system includes the organs that create human life. It's responsible for ensuring survival of the species.[30] It all starts with two cells.[31]

## Integumentary System

"Possible health effects of the skin include irritation, rash, redness or discoloration, dermatitis, and health effect related to other systems and organs due to contamination through the skin."[32]

---

[28] "Introduction to the Urinary System," SEER Training Module, National Institute of Health, National Cancer Institute, Accessed February 22, 2017. https://training.seer.cancer.gov/anatomy/urinary/.

[29] Agency for Toxic Substance and Disease Registry (ATSDR), Division of Health Assessment and Consultation, "Health Effects of Chemical Exposure," Accessed February 7, 2017: 2. https://www.atsdr.cdc.gov/emes/public/docs/Health%20Effects%20of%20Chemical%20Exposure%20FS.pdf.

[30] "Introduction to the Reproductive System," SEER Training Module, National Institute of Health, National Cancer Institute, Accessed February 22, 2017. https://training.seer.cancer.gov/anatomy/reproductive/.

[31] National Geographic, Human Body 101, Video, Accessed February 7, 2017, https://www.nationalgeographic.com/science/health-and-human-body/human-body/

[32] Agency for Toxic Substance and Disease Registry (ATSDR), Division of Health Assessment and Consultation, "Health Effects of Chemical Exposure," Accessed February 7, 2017: 3. https://www.atsdr.cdc.gov/emes/public/docs/Health%20Effects%20of%20Chemical%20Exposure%20FS.pdf.

This organ system includes skin, hair, and nails. It's responsible for covering the body to prevent germs from entering the body and damaging internal organs, and helping to maintain the immune system. Skin is the largest organ.[33]

The importance of each of these major organ systems is apparent in their descriptions. Living a healthy life requires that we protect and care for our bodies. While our bodies are amazing, they do have limitations. And we only receive one in a lifetime.

When cells are damaged, they prevent the body from functioning "normally" which could result in a multitude of health conditions.

The table below captures health conditions that were cited by more than 20 credible organizations, identifying the effects that chemicals may have on human health.

---

[33] "Healthy Skin," American Skin Association, Accessed March 7, 2017. http://www.americanskin.org/resource/

## Table 3: Illnesses that may be Caused by Chemicals in Everyday Products

| | |
|---|---|
| alcoholism | edema and fluid retention syndromes |
| allergic skin reaction | endocrine diseases |
| alopecia areata | endometriosis in adult women |
| Alzheimer's disease | enuresis |
| angina | eosinophilic gastroenteritis |
| angioedema | eye irritation |
| anxiety | fatigue |
| aphthous stomatitis | fibrocystic breast disease |
| arrhythmias | fibromyalgia |
| arthralgia | frequent colds |
| asthma | gastric and duodenal ulcers |
| attention deficit disorder | gastrointestinal diseases |
| attention deficit hyperactivity disorder | glomerulonephritis |
| autism | granulomatosis with polyangiitis (Wegener's) |
| autoimmune hemolytic anemia | graves' disease |
| autoimmune hepatitis | Guillain-Barré syndrome |
| behavioral problems in children | gut flora dysbiosis |
| bloody nose | headaches |
| cancer (several types) | hearing loss |
| cardiovascular diseases | hypertension |
| central nervous system damage | idiopathic thrombocytopenic purpura |
| certain anemias | immune deficiencies |
| certain malabsorption | infantile enterocolitis |

| | |
|---|---|
| syndromes | |
| certain pneumonias | infertility |
| chronic bronchitis | insulin resistance in adults |
| chronic cystitis | interfere with production or activity of hormones in endocrine system |
| chronic fatigue | irritability |
| chronic gastritis | irritable bowel syndrome |
| cognitive impairment (ability to mentally function, focus, think, remember) | kidney damage and diseases |
| conjunctivitis | laryngeal edema |
| death | lethargy, fatigue, feeling ill |
| declines in serum cholinesterase levels | leukemia (increased risk) |
| dermatitis herpetiformis | liver damage and diseases |
| dermatomyositis | loss of appetite |
| developmental disorders | loss of coordination |
| diabetes | lower IQs |
| dizziness | lung cancer |
| dyslexia (difficulty reading) | lupus erythematosus |
| dysmenorrhea | manic-depressive illness |
| dyspnea (difficult or labored breathing) | memory disorders |
| eating disorders | Meniere's disease |
| eczema | migraine headaches |
| multiple chemical sensitivity | recurrent vaginitis |
| multiple sclerosis | regional ileitis |
| muscle pain | reproductive problems and complications |
| muscle spasm headaches | respiratory diseases |
| myalgia | rheumatoid arthritis |
| myasthenia gravis | rhinitis |
| myocardial infarctions | schizophrenia |

| | |
|---|---|
| nasal congestion | scleroderma/systemic sclerosis |
| nausea | sensory organ diseases |
| nephrotic syndrome | serious illness |
| nervous system damage | sexual dysfunction |
| neurological diseases | sinusitis |
| nonhodgkins lymphoma (increased risk) | Sjögren's syndrome |
| nose and throat irritation | skin diseases |
| obesity | somatoform disorders |
| other arthritides | sore throat and cough |
| other health problems | spaciness |
| panic disorders | systemic lupus erythematosus |
| Parkinson's disease | thrombocytopenia |
| pemphigus/pemphigoid | thrombophlebitis |
| permanent damage to health | thyroid dysfunction |
| pernicious anemia | tinnitus |
| personality change | ulcerative colitis |
| polyarteritis nodosa | urticaria |
| Polymyositis | various cognitive |
| premenstrual syndrome | vasculitis |
| pressure in the ear | vertigo |
| primary biliary cirrhosis | vitiligo |
| psoriasis | vomiting |
| rashes | vulvodynia |
| recurrent otitis media | wheezing |

Let's look at a few of these health conditions, affecting so many people, in greater detail and what exactly is happening in the body's system.

## Auto Immune Disorders

Table 3 above is peppered with more than 20 auto immune disorders. Like Atari's Space Invaders, there is a constant state of attack. An autoimmune disorder develops when the immune system thinks healthy cells are invaders and it repeatedly attacks the healthy cells in an effort to protect the body.

*"More than 80 diseases occur as a result of the immune system attacking the body's own organs, tissues, and cells."*[34]

Autoimmune disorders can affect the entire body—heart, brain, nerves, muscles, skin, eyes, joints, lungs, kidneys, glands, digestive tract, and blood vessels.[35]

When free radicals damage cells, it can lead to autoimmune disease.[36]

## Multiple Chemical Sensitivity

This one is near and dear to my heart. Back in 2008, Multiple Chemical Sensitivity (MCS) was largely considered by the medical community to be a mental health issue. Statements about the auto immune disorder were similar to

---

[34] "Autoimmune Diseases," National Institute of Health, National Institute of Allergy and Infectious Diseases, Accessed March 9, 2017.
https://www.niaid.nih.gov/diseases-conditions/autoimmune-diseases
[35] "Understanding Autoimmune Diseases," U.S. Department of Human Services, National Institute of Health, National Institute of Arthritis and Musculoskeletal and Skin Diseases, March 2016: 1.
doi: NIH Publication No. 16–7582
https://www.niams.nih.gov/sites/default/files/catalog/files/understanding_aut oimmune.pdf
[36] "How Chemical Injury/Chemical Sensitivity Affects the Body (pg 2)," Chemical Injury.net, Accessed February 7, 2017,
http://www.chemicalinjury.net/html/how_chemical_injury_chemical_s1.html

those of multiple sclerosis (MS), fibromyalgia, and chiropractic treatment at one time—it only exists in your head; you only feel better when you THINK you do.

Thankfully, the larger medical community is starting to better understand the reality of MCS. Doctors specializing in environmental medicine generally understand the illness better than most.

MCS is an illness that causes individuals to react to even small chemical exposures, causing symptoms that range from unpleasant to temporary to permanently disabling. [37]

The Asthma and Allergy Foundation of America identified four categories for classifying chemical sensitivity:

> *"Annoyance Reactions.* These result from a heightened sensitivity to unpleasant odors, called olfactory awareness, in some susceptible individuals. Your ability to cope with offensive—but mostly nonirritating—odors has a lot to do with genetic or acquired factors, among which are infection and inflammation of the mucous membranes or polyps (growths of the nasal or sinus membranes), and abuse of tobacco and nasal decongestants.

> *"Irritational Syndromes.* These are caused by significant exposure to irritating chemicals that are more likely than others to penetrate the mucous membranes. These types of reactions can affect certain nerve endings and cause burning sensations in

---

[37] American Academy of Environmental Medicine
https://www.aaemonline.org/chemicalsensitivity.php

the nose, eyes, and throat. They usually come and go, and can be reversed.

*"Immune Hypersensitivity.* This is the basis of allergic diseases, such as allergic rhinitis (hay fever) and asthma. They are generally caused by naturally occurring organic chemicals found in pollens, molds, dust and animals. At present, only a relatively few industrial chemicals are known to have the capability of provoking a true immune system response. Among them are acid anhydrides and isocyanates and other chemicals that are able to bond to human proteins.

*"Intoxication Syndrome.* In some cases, long-term exposure to noxious chemicals may cause serious illness, or even death. Permanent damage to health may be the outcome of such reactions, which are dependent on the nature and extent of the chemical exposure. Toxic pollutants are given off by a number of building products, such as furniture, cleaning fluids, pesticides, and paints."[38]

Cancer

Every single person reading this has been touched by cancer—experienced it, helped a friend or family member through it, or lost a loved one to it.

The ATSDR *Chemicals, Cancer and You* booklet has an awesome graphic of what can happen to cells when they're

---

[38] Asthma and Allergy Foundation of America. "Chemical Sensitivities." Accessed November 14, 2015.

damaged by chemicals and lead to a medical condition.[39] The graphic below (Graphic 1) is my own variation.

Everyone should cut out this page (or copy it if it's not your book) and pin it to the refrigerator. Seriously.

It's a great reminder of what happens when our cells are injured by chemicals.

Graphic 1: Changes in Human Cells as a Result of Chemicals

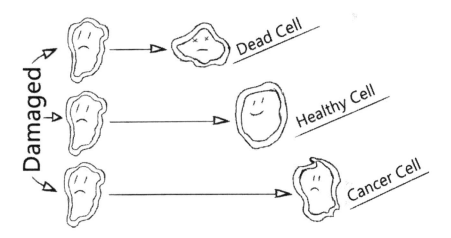

As you can see, when cells are damaged one of three things can result:
1) The damaged cell dies.
2) The damaged cell regenerates as a normal healthy cell.
3) The damaged cell regenerates as a damaged, or cancer, cell.

---

[39] Agency for Toxic Substance and Disease Registry (ATSDR), Division of Health Assessment and Consultation, "Chemicals, Cancer, and You," Accessed December 12, 2015: 5.
https://www.atsdr.cdc.gov/emes/public/docs/Chemicals,%20Cancer,%20and%20You%20FS.pdf

Simply put, the cells in our bodies are continuously producing cells and then dividing them so that we are continually generating new cells—every single day. Cells that are damaged by chemicals can have a change in their DNA, which can lead to cancer. This is further described in Dr. Ziem's research, which states that free radicals damage the DNA which can lead to cancer.[40]

In addition, when chemicals injure the cell's energy structure, it can lead to increased concentration of acid levels. Cells do not function normally in excessively acidic bodies.

*"Between 2010 and 2020, we [CDC] expect the number of new cancer cases in the United States to go up about 24% in men to more than 1 million cases per year, and by about 21% in women to more than 900,000 cases per year."*[41] The WHO expects the number of new cancer cases worldwide to rise by about 70% over the next 2 decades.[42]

With those odds, we are all affected in some way. *"More than 200 types of cancer have been identified. Many risk factors—such as age, genetics, or lifestyle choices—can add to your chance of getting cancer."*[43]

---

[40] "How Chemical Injury/Chemical Sensitivity Affects the Body (pg 2)," Chemical Injury.net, Accessed February 7, 2017, http://www.chemicalinjury.net/html/how_chemical_injury_chemical_s1.html

[41] "Expected New Cancer Cases and Deaths in 2020," Centers for Disease Control and Prevention, Page last reviewed: June 24, 2015. https://www.cdc.gov/cancer/dcpc/research/articles/cancer_2020.htm

[42] "Cancer," Fact sheet, World Health Organization, February 2017. http://www.who.int/mediacentre/factsheets/fs297/en/

[43] Agency for Toxic Substance and Disease Registry (ATSDR), Division of Health Assessment and Consultation, "Chemicals, Cancer, and You," Accessed December 12, 2015: 7.

Get this, though: according to Breastcancer.org, "About 85% of breast cancers occur in women who have no family history of breast cancer."[44]

Taking that one step further, "Research suggests that only five to ten percent of cancers are hereditary. That means the non-inherited causes of cancer—the lifestyle choices we make, the foods we eat, and our physical activity levels—have a direct impact on our overall cancer risk."[45]

There's a game changer.

Lifestyle choices can increase or REDUCE your chance of getting cancer.

Woohoo!!! YOU can do something. YOU can make choices that lessen your chances. YOU are a big factor in deciding your health! How exciting is that!?!?

And there's more.

The ATSDR goes on to say, "Cancer is usually not caused by only one risk factor but by several of them. The more risk factors you have, the higher your risk of getting cancer."[46]

---

https://www.atsdr.cdc.gov/emes/public/docs/Chemicals,%20Cancer,%20and%20You%20FS.pdf

[44] "U.S. Breast Cancer Statistics," BreastCancer.org, Last Modified January 9, 2018.
http://www.breastcancer.org/symptoms/understand_bc/statistics

[45] "Reduce Cancer Risk," Prevent Cancer Foundation, Accessed March 23, 2017.
https://preventcancer.org/learn/

[46] Agency for Toxic Substance and Disease Registry (ATSDR), Division of Health Assessment and Consultation, "Chemicals, Cancer, and You," Accessed December 12, 2015: 7.

So what do we do with this bit of valuable information?

We create a plan. A plan to, over time, reduce our exposure to chemicals. Make healthier choices. Create environments and lifestyles that may help you, your children, and family live healthier lives. And be incredibly grateful that we have the opportunity to do so.

Cellular changes don't happen overnight. Changes to cells occur in a series of steps that take a long time.[47]

### Short- & Long-Term Damage
Chemicals in everyday products can do short-term or long-term damage, or sometimes both. What starts out as short-term can lead to long-term health effects. It's worthwhile to listen to your body when you experience short-term health effects. Heed the warning to, hopefully, be able to avoid long-term consequences.

According to Dr. Ziem, the warning signs that our body gives us can differ depending on the types of chemicals we are exposed to and the individual themselves. Symptoms may get worse or more frequent as the exposure continues.

Short-term health effects are described below and broken into to two groups so that you can easily see the source of the information.

---

https://www.atsdr.cdc.gov/emes/public/docs/Chemicals,%20Cancer,%20and%20You%20FS.pdf

[47] Agency for Toxic Substance and Disease Registry (ATSDR), Division of Health Assessment and Consultation, "Chemicals, Cancer, and You," Accessed December 12, 2015: 2.
https://www.atsdr.cdc.gov/emes/public/docs/Chemicals,%20Cancer,%20and%20You%20FS.pdf.

## U.S. Environmental Protection Agency (EPA)[48]

- irritation of the eyes, nose, and throat
- headaches
- migraines
- dizziness or lightheaded
- fatigue

## Dr. Grace Ziem, Recognize Early Warning Signs[49]

- irritation and inflammation of the respiratory system including:
- burning
- soreness/irritation
- congestion
- painful ears, nose, sinuses, throat, voice box
- bronchi/chest/lungs
- short attention span or concentration
- difficulty with short term memory
- impaired coordination
- "pins and needles" feeling or numbness
- skin rash with burning
- chronic fatigue and/or aching
- frequent irritation/burning feeling in the stomach or esophagus area
- frequent gas/bloating

---

[48] "Introduction to Indoor Air Quality,' U.S. Environmental Protection Agency, Last Updated January 26, 2017.
https://www.epa.gov/indoor-air-quality-iaq/introduction-indoor-air-quality
[49] "Preventing Chemical Injury," Chemical Injury.net, Accessed February 8, 2017,
http://www.chemicalinjury.net/preventingchemicalinjury.htm

Long-term effects

Long-term health effects are those that we've already covered—lifelong medical conditions that can be chronic and life threatening.

Even in the womb our kids can be affected by chemicals, with lifelong impacts. Our tough little bundles of joy adapt to the effects of chemicals while still in the womb, which can result in medical conditions as an adult. Eventually, it catches up to each of us in a different way.

*"While the mother's body and the placenta offer protection from many things, some chemicals and radiation can reach the fetus. The developing fetus modifies its development to 'adapt' to these environmental cues. This adaptive ability is important for survival, but the permanent changes that result have also been linked to adult disease."*[50]

## **How Chemicals Enter the Body**

How do these little buggers of chemicals get into our systems? The University of Calgary Professor Tang G. Lee developed the Vital Signs curriculum[51] explaining three most common ways:

**Breathing** (inhalation) – This is where most of the contaminants enter our bodies. Since it's critical to survival

---

[50] "'Disrupted Development: The Dangers of Prenatal BPA Exposure," Breast Cancer Fund, September 2013: 5.
https://d124kohvtzl951.cloudfront.net/wp-content/uploads/2017/03/02025229/Report_Disrupted-Development-the-Dangers-of-Prenatal-BPA-Exposure_September_2013.pdf
[51] Professor Tang G. Lee. "Vital Signs, Health and the Built Environment: Indoor Air Quality." The University of Calgary. Accessed October 24, 2016 and January 19, 2018.
http://www.mtpinnacle.com/pdfs/iaq.pdf

that we breathe, we may want to look at how to change WHAT we're breathing in.

Let's get a little science crazy again. Gases affect our bodies the most. They come into our bodies through our nose and mouth, aka the respiratory system, and then are transferred into the blood stream and carried through our bodies.

What we breathe is distributed throughout our entire body. See Graphic 2 below. These contaminants come in the form of dusts, mists, fumes, vapors, and gas.[52] This not only causes respiratory problems but also neurological[53], physical[54] , and behavior disorders[55]. Particles that are larger in size enter our nose and mouths as well, but are typically caught by nose hairs and throat hairs (called cilia).

---

[52] "How Chemicals Enter the Body," University at Buffalo, The State University of New York, Accessed March 23, 2017.
https://www.buffalo.edu/facilities/ehs/training/right-to-know-training/how-chemicals-enter-the-body.html
[53] "Neurological Diseases and Disorders," National Institute of Environmental Health Sciences, Climate and Human Health, Last Reviewed July 20, 2017.
https://www.niehs.nih.gov/research/programs/geh/climatechange/health_imp acts/neurological_diseases/index.cfm
[54] "Chemicals and You," Environmental Health Center – Dallas, Accessed January 19, 2018.
https://www.ehcd.com/chemicals-and-you/
[55] "Deeper Understanding of Link between Chemical Pollutants and Autism," Autism Speaks, Accessed January 19, 2018.
https://www.autismspeaks.org/science/science-news/top-ten-lists/2012/deeper-understanding-link-chemical-pollutants-and-autism

Graphic 2: Chemicals Breathed - Travel Path

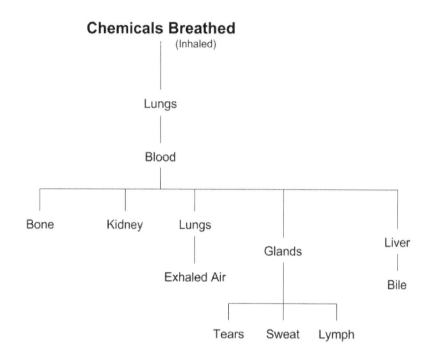

**Absorption** (through the skin) – The skin absorbs chemicals. Chemicals are absorbed through the three layers of skin, entering the blood stream and affecting several organs in the body. See Graphic 3. Chemicals can enter through direct contact with the eyes as well. Pretty straight forward.

Graphic 3: Chemicals Absorbed by Skin - Travel Path

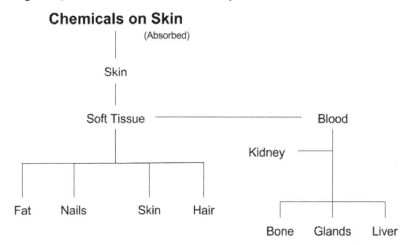

**Ingestion** (swallowing or eating them) – First off, eewwww... that was not in the curriculum. Eating foods and drinking liquids that have been exposed to chemicals can carry those chemicals into the body. The digestive and urinary systems break down and absorb the foods we eat and liquids we drink. The chemicals become absorbed into the blood system and circulate throughout the body.[56] See Graphic 4.

Sources of contaminants include chemical dusts, particles, and mists that are inhaled through the mouth and swallowed, or objects that may have been contaminated, such as hands, food, and cigarettes, that come in contact with the mouth.[57]

---

[56] Agency for Toxic Substance and Disease Registry (ATSDR), "Module Two, Routes of Exposure," Training Manual. Accessed January 19, 2018. https://www.atsdr.cdc.gov/training/toxmanual/pdf/module-2.pdf

[57] "How Chemicals Enter the Body," University at Buffalo, The State University of New York, Accessed March 23, 2017. https://www.buffalo.edu/facilities/ehs/training/right-to-know-training/how-chemicals-enter-the-body.html

Graphic 4: Chemicals Swallowed - Travel Path

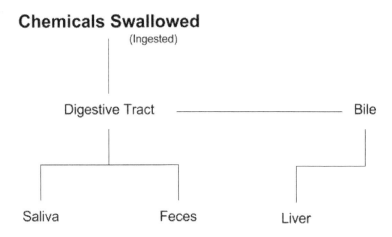

Graphics 2 through 4, based on the Vital Signs curriculum[58], are great visuals for understanding exactly how the chemicals enter and travel through our bodies.

Given all of this information, you may be wondering how much in medical bills and loss of productivity is associated with health conditions that may be caused by chemicals.

"The researchers found that the U.S. spends more than $340 billion each year on health care related to exposure to hormone disrupting chemicals, such as flame retardants and

---

[58] Professor Tang G. Lee. "Vital Signs, Health and the Built Environment: Indoor Air Quality." The University of Calgary. Accessed October 24, 2016 and January 19, 2018.
http://www.mtpinnacle.com/pdfs/iaq.pdf

pesticides, and that exposure causes the loss of almost 13 million IQ points."[59]

"To put those figures into perspective, this year's budget for the Pentagon was $605 billion, while the Medicare budget was $583 billion."[60]

That's a significant chunk of change. So how do we fix this problem? For starters, by taking it seriously.

We often shrug illness off as something that "just happens," dismissing it as normal. We feel bad for kids with constant runny noses, raise money for people fighting cancer, and hold the door for women and men with MS. But it never occurs to us that the cause might be the clothes we're wearing, our choice of shampoo, or our freshly remodeled home.

While empathy, resources, and kindness are so incredibly important, they are not enough. Change, real life-altering lifestyle change, is needed.

---

[59] Alex Formuzis and Violet Batcha, "IQs Plummet and Healthcare Costs Surge From Endocrine Disrupting Chemicals", EWG News and Analysis, October 20, 2016. https://www.ewg.org/enviroblog/2016/10/iqs-plummet-and-healthcare-costs-surge-endocrine-disrupting-chemicals#.WIldJKinHIU

[60] Alex Formuzis and Violet Batcha, "IQs Plummet and Healthcare Costs Surge From Endocrine Disrupting Chemicals", EWG News and Analysis, October 20, 2016. https://www.ewg.org/enviroblog/2016/10/iqs-plummet-and-healthcare-costs-surge-endocrine-disrupting-chemicals#.WIldJKinHIU

# Chapter 3
# Our Amazing Bodies

Our bodies are truly amazing. They can heal themselves—heal the damaged cells—if they are given the opportunity to do so. How do we give our bodies the opportunity to heal?

By creating an environment with the least amount of chemicals as possible.

There is no magic pill to reverse cell damage. Although sometimes I wish there were.

Dr. Grace Ziem M.D., Dr. P.H., who has been practicing medicine for over 38 years and is the founder of ChemicalInjury.net,[61] calls the cycle of damaging cells "chronic damage to body biochemistry."[62] She goes on to state that "unless and until this biochemistry is healed

---

[61] "About Dr. Grace Ziem," Chemical Injury.net, Accessed February 7, 2017, http://www.chemicalinjury.net/biosketch.htm

[62] "Neutral Sensitization: The Medical Key to Treatment of Chemical Injury," Chemical Injury.net, Accessed February 7, 2017, http://www.chemicalinjury.net/html/neural_sensitization__the_medi.html

naturally, inflammation and ongoing damage will occur. Drugs cannot heal these vicious cycles."[63]

Cellular damage is difficult to reverse, but it can be done naturally.

I've done it. I have not achieved 100% perfection, but I have been able to improve my health.

As I began to live life with fewer chemicals, the number of sinus infections decreased from 88% of the time to only a few per year.

And then to zero.

It's been four years since I've had a sinus infection. It's been four years since my son has had a sinus infection.

What a stark contrast to the chronic sinusitis that we lived with for nearly eight years.

When I first started working towards living life with fewer chemicals, my son was eight years old. I was a single parent in the truest of forms. Between working full time, attending college to finish my Bachelor's degree, maintaining our house, raising my son, and socializing with family and friends, my days were filled. After earning my degree, I worked two jobs.

That has been my lifestyle for over 10 years.

---

[63] "Neutral Sensitization: The Medical Key to Treatment of Chemical Injury," Chemical Injury.net, Accessed February 7, 2017, http://www.chemicalinjury.net/html/neural_sensitization__the_medi.html

Like many of you, I didn't have a lot of extra time on my hands. While I understood that chemical injury wouldn't be fixed with medication, I needed a solution that would allow me to make large life changes in smaller manageable steps.

Like many of you, I too didn't have the money, time, or energy to add something else to my life. My resources were fully committed.

But it was a change that I chose to make. For myself. For my son. For our future.

And I was able to do it without giving up the things that were most important to me. And you can too.

There are a few overarching strategies that are important to living life with fewer chemicals. Really, these strategies can be applied to any type of health improvement goals. They require a shift in thinking and can help avoid common pitfalls that sometimes happen when working towards a big goal.

## Want To, Not Must Do

The beautiful, magnificent thing about life is that you and I— each of us every day—get to make choices. In the lyrics of Rush's *Freewill*, "...if you choose not to decide, you still have made a choice..." You've made the choice to do nothing; the choice to avoid action. As you and I know, burying your head in the sand to avoid reality doesn't make the situation go away or get better. It just prolongs the inevitable.

Of course, you haven't read this far to prolong action. You're ready to make a change in your life.

The specific action and steps that you take to living life with fewer chemicals will be your choice, throughout your life and throughout this book. Each chapter will have several strategies for each reader—no matter where you are in life. Newly beginning your journey or approaching super star status, living life with fewer chemicals is a series of small steps that can make a large impact on your life.

No one can or should be telling you what's right for you. You own your opinions and feelings. If along the way you feel this isn't the right time for you to live a healthier lifestyle, then this book (and other resources) will be there when you're ready to make your health and the health of your family a priority.

If this IS the time—YOUR TIME—to live a healthier life with fewer chemicals, then take a few minutes to celebrate that!

And then start redefining what healthy means to you.

## Redefine What Healthy Is

When you think of healthy, what do you think of? Eating, exercise, a good night's sleep, work-life balance, low stress, and mental wellness are likely the topics that come to mind. Add to that, living life with fewer chemicals. How in the h-e-doublehockeysticks do you do that? We do it together.

Living healthy is more than eating right and exercising. It's more than getting a good night's sleep and lowering stress. It's about avoiding chemicals that may be damaging our bodies—protecting and taking care of the one body we are given.

Over time, as I learned about chemicals in our everyday products, my definition of healthy changed, and it will change for you too.

My definition of healthy evolved from:
- eating healthy
- exercising
- sleeping eight hours
- spiritual activity
- getting together with friends and family (social)
- learning one new thing every week (growth)
- spending time with my son

to:
- living life with fewer chemicals
- eating healthy organic foods
- exercising
- sleeping nine hours
- spiritual activity
- wearing nontoxic clothing
- living in a home with nontoxic building materials, furnishings, and household items
- getting together with friends and family (social)
- learning one new thing every week (growth)
- spending time with my son

Redefine what your definition of healthy is. That new definition of healthy that includes living life with fewer chemicals will help you achieve your overarching goal.

As you learn strategies for avoiding chemicals in everyday products, you'll take steps towards the overarching goal that we all have in common—living life with fewer chemicals.

After you set this big goal, it'll become the overarching measurement for success. For now, that's all you need. You'll each set smaller goals as you work through this book.

The three most important things to remember are 1) the big goal is to live life with fewer chemicals, 2) healthy means living life with fewer chemicals, and 3) taking small steps, one step at a time, will help you get there.

You will know what steps are working well by paying attention to patterns.

## Pay Attention to Patterns

Our ever amazing bodies "talk" to us constantly. Comprised of systems that function around the clock, heal our wounds, and fight to keep us healthy, our bodies are constantly sending signals to our brain telling us what it needs. It is making us aware of things of pleasure and displeasure, sources of stress and distress, and causes of illness.

If we listen—actually listen—to what our bodies are telling us, we can make choices that help instead of hurt our health. When you honor your body it will function even better.

When I first read the list of symptoms associated with chemical exposures, I thought to myself, these symptoms could be caused by nearly ANYTHING. How am I going to know if it's the chemicals or the stomach flu? Or stress? Or sleep deprivation? Or any number of other things?

It's a valid question, and one that I have been asked many times.

Patterns, that's how. You know by listening to your body, and paying close attention to cause and effect. By paying attention to the patterns.

Yoga instructors are infamous for teaching people to listen to and respect their body. They teach students to pay attention to how they feel when they do a certain yoga move.

Applied life-wide, pay attention to how you feel when you eat certain foods or do certain activities. How does your body feel when you are in different environments?

In the case of chemicals, there are patterns that tend to show themselves.

Over the years, indoor shopping malls have been a trigger for symptoms in some people. Dizzy, lightheaded, tired, and fatigued (that day or the following day) are some of the symptoms they have experienced. These individuals can feel completely fine, shop anywhere from five minutes to several hours (depending on the individual), and experience the same symptoms each time. When they go back a day later, a week later, or two months later, the exact same symptoms happen.

Some patterns are harder to identify. They're buried under layers and layers of symptoms. In my experience, there were products affecting me that I didn't even realize were affecting me until I started to eliminate products with chemicals in them.

Before we moved in 2009, my body was always swollen. I'd wake up in the morning and fold my hands together and feel my fingers squeeze by one another. My feet would hit the floor and the swelling would get worse as I walked barefoot on the laminate wood floor. If I didn't put socks on, my feet would swell to the point of hurting when I walked.

At first I thought my body was just swollen due to typical "life" activities that every parent experiences—some sleep deprived nights, an occasional pizza as we're running out the door, the stress of working and raising a child. Of course, in hindsight, it sounds silly to think that was the cause of the extreme swelling, but, hey, as we grow older, we all complain more about aches and pains. It was par for the course. Welcome to adulthood.

As I started paying close attention and listening to my body, it became clear to me that the swollen-feet-to-the-point-of-pain-when-walking was being caused by the flooring. Socks made a difference. And socks were not a cure for aging aches and pains. That's when I first started noticing patterns and paying attention to cause and effect. It's helped me in incredible ways ever since.

After I cracked the case of the painfully swollen feet, it was clear to me that something was causing the general swelling, but I had no idea what. Understanding or "listening to" our bodies is a process of finding those patterns, fixing them, and uncovering more patterns to fix.

It's a process that most people don't take the time to pay attention to. And for good reason. We are taught not to.

**Real Strength**
From childhood on we're taught to push through the tough times and be strong. Many people think of strength as pushing through, persevering, giving blood, sweat, and tears

to whatever you're doing. And sometimes that type of strength is needed.

Pushing through IS important. Persevering makes us feel proud and powerful. But what if you're doing it at the expense of your health?

The real strength comes in knowing your true limits—pushing yourself to grow without sacrificing your health. Strength is not ignoring signs, symptoms, or episodes. It's facing them head on and doing something about it.

All too often parents, friends, and colleagues tell us to push through. Go to work sick (and infect the rest of the office) to show you're not a wimp. Eat the mega uber gigantic burger exploding with mouth-watering toppings to be the best burger-eater ever. Fill your schedule with work, sports, school, friends, and family outings until you have no down time left for yourself just so that people don't call you lazy. Ignore your chronic illness symptoms—after all, everyone gets sick. Everyone's allergies are worse. Everyone's getting cancer. Power through and you'll be fine.

Except, that strategy is not working.

Strength in this case is pushing *change*. Standing up to the "norm." Joining the growing group of people that are saying enough is enough and taking back their health by living life with fewer chemicals.

You. Are. Important. Your HEALTH is important. Recognizing that and taking action is a life-changing moment.

**Action!**
I'd love to have a health condition that makes me feel sick all of the time!

... said no one. Ever.

Then take action!

I'm not gonna lie. It won't be as easy as popping pills or snapping your fingers. Living life with less chemicals sounds scary and exhausting. It can be overwhelming. Shut-down, give up, don't-care overwhelming. I get it. I've been there.

But it is manageable. It can be done. Easily. If you just take it one step at a time...

Allow yourself to take...

One.
Step.
At.
A.
Time.

Until one day you look back and realize just how far you've come. How great you feel. How great your family feels. And how your life has changed for the better.

The difference between taking action and not taking action (aside from the obvious) is this: by not taking action you are saying to yourself, "I recognize the problem but am not going to take control of my health. I'm too scared or don't want to put in the effort to live life with fewer chemicals, and I don't mind if I have health issues during my time on Earth."

By taking action you are saying to yourself, "I recognize the problem and I am taking control of my health! I'm taking steps to live life with fewer chemicals in order to live a healthier life during the time I have on this Earth."

And you are well on your way to doing that.

You now understand that there are chemicals in our everyday products and that they may be harming people's health. You've set the big goal of living life with fewer chemicals. Now we'll talk about what small steps to take to get there.

# Chapter 4
# Food

Food, glorious food!

I used to think eating was just something that was necessary to survive. Of course, it IS necessary for survival... and so much more.

The food that we eat can make or break our day. What we eat can make us feel bloated and ill, foggy-brained, slow and groggy, scattered, cold, pukey, gassy, achy, mad, tired, irritated, and edgy. OR happy, clear, focused, energized, warm, peppy, alive, and comfortable. It can cause us to do well on tests... or not so much and even lower IQ levels.[64]

What we eat can improve our mood. When I started eating organic food, I noticed a difference in my own mood and so did those around me. Which was (and still is!) appreciated by all!

---

[64] Michael Warhurst, "It's a No Brainer! Action needed to stop children being exposed to chemicals that harm their brain development!," March 7, 2017. http://www.chemtrust.org/brain/

What was in our non-organic food that could have caused this?

You guessed it. Chemicals. In ways that I didn't expect.

"Chemicals are used in every step of the process that puts food on our table: production, harvesting, processing, packing, transport, marketing and consumption and can be dangerous to our health." – Physicians for Social Responsibility[65]

Let's look at these categories a little closer to understand how chemicals can get into the food supply.

## Production and Harvesting

What do we mean by production and harvesting? It's the growing of food, as in farming.

When farmers grow crops, they are growing and caring for our food supply—the very food that gives us fuel and energy to live. During the growing season, farmers spray fertilizers and pesticides onto the fields in order to help crops grow or to kill bugs, insects, and other pests that are eating the crops. It's understandable. Farmers may feel the need to protect their food supply and maximize their return on investment, so they spray chemicals on the food.

Except, the added chemicals such as pesticides and fertilizers are ending up IN our food.

---

[65] "Toxic Chemicals in our Food System," Fact Sheet, Physicians for Social Responsibility. Accessed February 13, 2017: 1.
http://www.psr.org/assets/pdfs/toxic-chemicals-in-our-food.pdf

In fact, products on the grocery store shelves are made with pesticide-filled and fertilizer-filled food, unless they specifically state "organic."

Foods that are sprayed with pesticides and fertilizers are offered as "healthy" fruits and vegetables in the produce section of a grocery store and may be used by grocery store deli departments to prepare salad bars and deli dishes.

Food manufacturers use wheat, corn, rye, and other food ingredients that have been sprayed with chemicals in order to make chips, crackers, tortilla shells, soups, and salsa.

The same crops being sprayed with pesticides and fertilizers are used to feed animals that produce milk and meat. Cheese, yogurt, sour cream, butter, pork chops, ground beef, steaks, chicken, turkey, ham—these are all products that can contain chemicals that animals have been exposed to prior to production.

Even my favorite combination of vegetables—peas-n-corn, which comes in frozen, canned, or fresh varieties—can contain chemicals.

As you and I eat these foods, pesticides and other chemicals travel from our mouths to our stomachs through our digestive systems and throughout our blood supply.

We serve this food for dinner, feeding it to our kids, spouses, sisters, brothers, parents, and ourselves.

Let me ask you this: Would you add a pinch of pesticide to your veggie dish before you serve it? Or top the fruit dessert with fertilizer before you serve it to your family?

How about a few drops into a nice hot cup of coffee or tea to start your morning? Ahhh, drinking the refreshing pesticides being released into the hot drink, sliding down your throat into your stomach for your whole body to absorb.

Sounds ridiculous, doesn't it? Turns out, that's what's happening. Except that the pesticides, fertilizer, and other chemicals are added by others. *We're* not adding pesticides into our dinner, but during processing the farmers are adding it—not to purposely poison us, but to kill the pests and to grow food faster.

While you're not adding a few drops of poison, it's still ending up on our dinner tables. Just because you yourself didn't put it there doesn't mean that it's not there.

**Processing**
How about in manufacturing? This is the manufacturing of food, as in making and assembling.

Think of canned, boxed, and packaged products that are typically found in the middle aisles of a grocery store. In addition to chemicals during harvesting, packaged food can have synthetic additives, preservatives, and sweeteners that are intentionally added to food. Why would this be? To change the color, texture, thickness, appearance, and taste of the food.

"Many studies have shown that food dyes can impair children's behavior, but until now the amounts of dyes in packaged foods has been a secret. New research by Purdue University scientists, published in the journal *Clinical Pediatrics*, reports on the dye content of scores of breakfast cereals, candies, baked goods, and other foods. According to the nonprofit Center for Science in the Public Interest, the findings are disturbing since the amounts of dyes found in even single servings of numerous foods—or combinations of several dyed foods—are higher than the levels demonstrated in some clinical trials to impair some children's behavior."[66]

What are these artificial additives and sweeteners made of? You guessed it, chemicals.

As Kris Carr stated in *Crazy, Sexy Diet,* "Artificial sweeteners are potent nerve toxins and never should have been approved as safe for human consumption. They have the potential to freak out and damage your nervous system—your brain and nerves—leading to a variety of symptoms from migraine headaches to unexplained seizures, dizziness, depression and vision problems.  They are even linked to cancer, obesity and diabetes."[67]

Kris Carr goes on to state, "I bet you didn't realize how many of these human-made tasty toxins you gobble up on a daily basis. They hide out in thousands of your favorite foods, including diet meals, flavored waters, popular drink mixes such as Crystal Light, many commercial salad dressings, and—ready for this?—even over-the-counter medicines like Alka-Seltzer, toothpastes, gum, vitamins, and those Listerine breath strips! Even the stuff that 'tastes like sugar because

---

[66]"First-ever Study Reveals Amounts of Food Dyes in Brand-name Foods: Amounts in Some Foods Exceed Levels Used in Many Tests of Dyes' Impact on Children's Behavior," Center for Science in the Public Interest, May 7, 2014. https://cspinet.org/new/201405071.html

[67] Kris Carr, *Crazy, Sexy Diet* (Connecticut: Globe Pequot Press, 2011), 48.

it's made from sugar' is highly processed and has been laced with chlorine."[68]

There are full departments dedicated to creating and adding chemicals to our food products. In fact, manufacturers may be adding these chemicals to hook people—so that people become addicted to their food product. It's actually fascinating and disturbing at the same time.

Food manufacturers, it appears, are using the principals of the tobacco industry in adding chemicals that are addictive. In order to understand this concept better, watch an excerpt from *The C Word*, a movie about beating cancer. The movie (and excerpt), narrated by Morgan Freeman, can be found on Robyn O'Brien's website.[69] O'Brien is a well-known advocate for the "new food economy."

To be clear, I'm not saying nicotine from cigarettes is in food. But I am saying there may be other, similarly addictive chemicals being added.

In fact, the U.S. Food and Drug Administration (FDA) created a list of over 4,000 chemicals that are added to foods that are on our tables, in our refrigerators, in our cabinets— that we eat every single day. And according to the FDA, that's a partial list. Over 4k! Good grief.

---

[68] Kris Carr, *Crazy, Sexy Diet* (Connecticut: Globe Pequot Press, 2011), 48.
[69] The C Word Movie. *Think Big Tobacco Is Bad? Look at Big Food.* Video. Directed by Meghan L. O'Hara. Performed by Morgan Freeman. 2016. Zorro and Me Films Production. Accessed on Robyn O'Brien "Morgan Freeman Shows Us How Big Tobacco Became Big Food." February 1, 2017. https://robynobrien.com/morgan-freeman-shows-us-how-big-tobacco-became-big-food/

It's easy to dismiss by thinking "it's not in my food supply" or "it's probably not in the food that I buy."

These chemicals have been found in popular food brands such as Kraft, Pillsbury, Sara Lee, Smucker's, Tyson, Wonder, and others, in foods such as macaroni and cheese, soups, drinks, etc. There are too many foods and manufacturers to list them all here.

"According to ingredient data obtained for a new food database project that is due out later this year, EWG researchers found azodicarbonamide, an industrial 'chemical foaming agent,' on the labels of many well-known brands, including Pillsbury, Sara Lee, Shoprite, Safeway, Smucker's, Fleischman's, Jimmy Dean, Kroger, Little Debbie, Tyson and Wonder."[70]

"Flame retardant, Brominated vegetable oil (BVO)... is also found in citrus-flavored sodas and sports drinks from the US."[71] It has been found in Mountain Dew, Sunkist, Powerade, Fanta, Gatorade, Fresca, Squirt, and has been linked to major organ damage, birth defects, growth problems, schizophrenia, and hearing loss. BVO also competes with iodine for receptor sites in the body, which

---

[70] "'Yoga Mat' Chemicals Found in nearly 500 Foods," Environmental Working Group, Updated February 28, 2014.
https://www.ewg.org/release/yoga-mat-chemical-found-nearly-500-foods#.Wll8h6inHlU
[71] "10 Banned Foods Americans Should Stop Eating," The Food Revolution Network, October 2, 2014.
https://foodrevolution.org/blog/10-banned-foods-americans-stop-eating/

can lead to iodine deficiency, hypothyroidism, autoimmune disease, and cancer.[72]

Powerade, Gatorade, Kraft, Smucker's, Tyson. These are the creators of foods that I was feeding to my son when he was a toddler and grade-schooler. These are the foods my family and friends were eating.

The fact of the matter is that if you're not buying organic, these chemicals are in your food supply. They may be affecting you and your family.

## Packaging

Packaging is another source for chemicals that can get into our food supply. You'd think that packaging wouldn't be that significant, but scientists have found that it is significant— chemicals from packaging are showing up in blood tests and labs.

In fact, 93% of Americans have detectable levels of BPA (a chemical found in plastic and food packaging) in their bodies, according to the U.S. Centers for Disease Control and Prevention.

"Eating food from cans—which are coated with a BPA polymer that leaches into food—is a major route of human exposure."[73]

---

[72] "10 Banned Foods Americans Should Stop Eating," The Food Revolution Network, October 2, 2014.
https://foodrevolution.org/blog/10-banned-foods-americans-stop-eating/
[73] "'Disrupted Development: The Dangers of Prenatal BPA Exposure," Breast Cancer Fund, September 2013: 3.
https://d124kohvtzl951.cloudfront.net/wp-content/uploads/2017/03/02025229/Report_Disrupted-Development-the-Dangers-of-Prenatal-BPA-Exposure_September_2013.pdf

Chemicals from plastic packaging are leaching into the food supply, and adding chemicals to whatever food is being stored in the plastic container. While the FDA's partial list of chemicals added to food tallies over 4,000, that list does not include chemicals from packaging.

This tally does.

According to the Environmental Working Group, "More than 10,000 additives[74] are allowed in food. Some are *direct additives* that are deliberately formulated into processed food. Others are *indirect additives* that get into food during processing, storage and packaging."[75]

Take a minute to digest that fact.

The easiest way to think about packaged products is to picture the center aisles of a grocery store. Each type of packaging comes with its own set of chemicals. Boxes, cans, bags, and plastic containers are all housing food for consumption.

Plastics are widely used to contain cereals, juices, crackers, soups (aluminum cans are lined with plastic), fruits, baking

---

[74] Author's Note: "By food additives, we mean substances that are added to food products and their packaging. Under federal law, the term 'food additive' is used to describe just one category of these substances, but we are using the term as it is commonly understood."

[75] "EWG's Dirty Dozen Guide to Food Additives," Environmental Working Group, November, 12, 2014. https://www.ewg.org/research/ewg-s-dirty-dozen-guide-food-additives?gclid=CjwKEAiAz4XFBRCW87vj6-28uFMSJAAHeGZbgEvzi_SxO4-WHgqQ0eOblQULww_ubP-CHplQ_hUyZBoCLPLw_wcB#.Wll-XKinHIU

goods, cooking oils, and so much more. Food absorbs what's in the air or space around it.

Think of what happens when you leave food uncovered in the fridge. It ends up tasting like "refrigerator," and then typically ends up in the garbaaaahhge. Same thing happens with chemicals from packaging, except that we don't usually taste them.

You might have heard the chemical name BPA, one of the hot-topic chemicals found in plastics, and for good reason—it's one of the common chemicals showing up in the blood supply of people of all ages—newborn to elderly.

I'm not going to bore you with a list of the over 10k chemicals found in foods, or suggest that you scour every single label for each chemical name. What a nightmare that would be!

It wouldn't help anyway. Manufacturers are not required to list chemicals on product labels.

Yeah. Crazy, right!?

Food manufacturers have argued against legislation requiring that ingredient labels include all ingredients, stating that ingredients are a trade secret. I can understand trade secret protection; what I can't understand is why some companies feel threatened by transparent labeling and others do not.

Truthfully, if hiding ingredients that are harmful to people's health are the types of trade secrets a company wants to keep, then I don't want to buy their product.

## Transport

Food absorbs what's in the environment—what's in the air, ground, and soil. The farther the food travels, the increased chance it has of absorbing more chemicals.

"The average American meal travels around fifteen hundred miles to get to the table. This means that when you sit down to your dinner of chicken, broccoli, and potatoes, each of these foods has traveled on average nearly fifteen hundred miles, by boat, train, plane or truck to get from the farm where it was grown to your dinner plate."[76]

As we discussed, packaging leaches chemicals into our food supplies. During hot months, as the transportation truck becomes warm from the heat and sun, the packaging heats up, off-gassing chemicals even faster than in its unheated state, causing even more chemicals to potentially leach into the food supplies.

During travel, vehicle exhaust may contribute to the chemicals that your food is exposed to.

Have you ever stopped too close to another vehicle in a traffic jam and the smell of exhaust consumes your vehicle, even when your windows are rolled up? Or are driving through a heavily concentrated downtown area on a day when the air is heavy and stagnant? Exhaust can be prevalent in the air during transportation.

---

[76] Marco Borges, *The 22-Day Revolution.* (New York: Celebra, a division of Penguin Group, 2015).

## Consumption

When eating food we sometimes use our hands. Not as
unrefined cavemen, but as a matter of eating convenience
foods while on the go. Finger foods, snacks, sandwiches, and
licorice are all examples of the many types of food we eat
with our hands instead of utensils.

Whatever is on your hands—pollen, grease, gasoline, dirt,
germs—sticks to your food and is popped into your mouth
when you eat. That food (and whatever was on your hands)
then travels through your digestive system.

The same goes for airborne contaminates like spray cleaners
or construction dust. If you're eating food in an area where
these contaminates are being released, your food may have a
little extra something on it.

## Marketing – Store Shelves

In a nutshell, "store shelves" take into consideration store
maintenance and sale-ability of food and merchandise.

Cleaners are sprayed or wiped onto the shelves where the
fruits and vegetables sit. Dish soap is used to clean doughnut
trays and deli bowls. Well, okay, if you're worried about
cleaners on doughnut trays, we may need to tackle the larger
topic of eating doughnuts. That's for another time.

Spray cleaners can spray too much. They have a reach that
goes beyond the original target. It's called "overspray."
Clever.

When cleaners are sprayed onto a shelf, they can also land on
the food surrounding the area being cleaned. In addition, the

food that was on the shelf will be going right back onto the shelf, sitting on cleaning chemical residue.

At closing, grocery stores clean shelves, check-out line conveyer belts, floors, cooking equipment in the deli, and meat slicers. Of course, you DO want those items to be cleaned. That would be super gross if they weren't. But you want them to be cleaned with less-chemical cleaners.

Flower departments in grocery stores are lovely and oh-so convenient for a spur-of-the-moment gesture. They may not be so good for our health though. Flowers and the water they're sitting in are often pumped with preservatives and sprayed with aerosol hair spray to make them last longer. Dyes are added to brighten or change the coloring on some flowers, from white to vivid blue or bright pink.

These are all opportunities for chemicals to further enter our food supplies through the air and by contact.

## Marketing – Environment Purchasing

Think about your grocery store purchasing experience. Where do you typically shop for food?

Organic food is becoming more available to consumers and being sold in various types of stores. Health conscious grocery stores that focus on carrying organic and healthier foods, standard grocery stores carrying food with the occasional organic section, and big box stores that carry a variety of merchandise including food, some of which is organic.

Standard grocery stores and big box stores now have organic sections or organic products mixed among non-organic products. Organic food is becoming more readily available to people.

While big box stores such as Costco, Sam's Club, Walmart, Target, and Meijer's carry organic foods, they also dedicate a large portion of the store to non-food products such as electronics, clothing, furniture, cleaners, plants, and decorations—products that typically contain chemicals harmful to people's health (as you'll read more about later).

Just for kicks, walk into a health-focused grocery store and smell the air. Pay attention to how the air smells when you walk in, and even when you walk through the cleaner aisle. One day later, visit a standard grocery store such as Pick 'n Save or Piggly Wiggly and smell the air when you walk in, and when you walk through the cleaning aisle. A day or two later visit a big box store, smelling the air when you walk in and when you walk down the cleaning aisle.

Did you notice a difference? The amount of cleaners and other chemicals that you smell are enormously different in each type of store, in my experience. The traditional grocery and big box stores typically had a stronger fragrance and stronger chemical smell, particularly the cleaner aisles, whereas the health-conscious stores typically had a far less chemical smell.

Not all chemicals that are harmful to people's health have a fragrance or smell to them, but for our purposes of explaining this point, we'll stick with fragranced products.

Plastic packaging and food are porous and absorb chemicals from the surrounding environment.

When stores carry products that are off-gassing chemicals into the air, such as cleaners, electronics, garden centers, clothing, and furniture, those chemicals could be absorbed into the packaging and food.

Let's look at a real-life example.

A few months ago a friend suggested that I buy organic food from a big box store in order to lower our grocery bill. Wanting to go with the flow, I optimistically gave it a try and bought a frozen organic vegetable blend from a big box store that we'll call Xyz for the purposes of this book.

When I arrived home I threw the bag of veggies into the freezer, my clothes in the basement washing machine, and jumped into the shower. A half an hour later, after my clothes had finished washing, I opened the freezer and noticed the smell of cleaners.  Odd, I thought.

Immediately, I wondered what I did differently. The frozen veggies were from Xyz. That was the only variable that had changed. Not a big deal, though. I dumped the veggies into two one-gallon closable bags and threw the original bag into the trash outside. An hour later, I opened the freezer again and the smell was completely gone. Lesson learned.

More importantly, what do we do with these lessons? How do we easily avoid food with chemicals in them while sticking to a budget and lifestyle that works well for each of us?

## **Solutions!**

There are several factors to take into account when buying food with fewer chemicals. The best strategy is to tackle the big overarching ways to avoid chemicals first, and then refine with details.

**USDA Organic Label**
Look for the USDA Organic label, and buy those products.

Not all organic is equally organic. The U.S. Department of Agriculture (USDA) has four classifications for organic: 100% Organic, Organic, "Made With" Organic, and Specific Organic Ingredients.

Products with the USDA Organic label have been certified by an accredited certifying agency and contain 95-100% organic content. The label below is theeeee label to look for. It takes the guess work out of knowing what products are nearly or entirely all organic. Thank you, USDA.[77]

Products that contain less than 95% organic content are *not* certified USDA organic.[78]

<hr>

[77] United States Department of Agriculture, USDA National Organic Program. "Labeling Organic Products," December 2016: 1.
https://www.ams.usda.gov/sites/default/files/media/Labeling%20Organic%20Products.pdf
[78] United States Department of Agriculture, USDA National Organic Program. "Labeling Organic Products," December 2016: 1.
https://www.ams.usda.gov/sites/default/files/media/Labeling%20Organic%20Products.pdf

## Read the Advertising Carefully

Food that is partly organic can say "made with" in small print, "ORGANIC" in big print across the top of the box, and return to small print to say the ingredient, like "wheat." Meaning this product contains only organic wheat, with the remainder of the ingredients being non-organic.

To the shopper racing through the aisles short on time, the word "organic" jumps out. This is a better alternative, but not a fully organic product.

Products containing at least 70% organic content may be labeled as "made with" and list up to three specified organic ingredients. It cannot be labeled with the USDA organic seal.[79]

## Scan the Ingredients List

Scan the ingredient label for just one simple word—organic.

This will tell you just how many ingredients are indeed organic. Organic ingredients will have the word "organic" before the ingredient. For example, organic wheat, organic olive oil, organic yeast, organic chicken—you get the idea.

Products containing less than 70% organic content can only list organic ingredients in the ingredients list and may not market the product as organic.[80]

---

[79] United States Department of Agriculture, USDA National Organic Program. "Labeling Organic Products," December 2016: 2.
https://www.ams.usda.gov/sites/default/files/media/Labeling%20Organic%20Products.pdf
[80] United States Department of Agriculture, USDA National Organic Program. "Labeling Organic Products," December 2016: 2.
https://www.ams.usda.gov/sites/default/files/media/Labeling%20Organic%20Products.pdf

When a product is certified organic, the criteria is focused on the food ingredients themselves and takes into account the growing, processing, and manufacturing stages of food production. This means the USDA-accredited certifying agencies are attesting that the food is 95-100% free of pesticides and fertilizers, added colors, thickeners, sweeteners, or manufactured synthetic (man-made) chemicals.

The USDA Organic seal is super easy to look for and a good indicator of products with significantly fewer chemicals in them.

But it does not take into account the packaging that the food is packaged in.

**Non-Plastic Packaging**
Simply put, avoid plastic packaging.

Plastic or plastic lined packaging is easy to identify but a bit tricky to avoid completely, simply due to the wide use of plastic. So we do what we can with the options we're presented. There are several foods and drinks that have a non-plastic packaged option and are easy to find.

Fruits and vegetables, juices, spaghetti sauce, olive oil, coconut oil, milk, salsa, peanut butter, jelly, and spices are a few examples of the foods that grocery stores, particularly health-focused stores, typically carry in a non-plastic packaging option. Typically these items are either unpackaged (in the case of fruits and veggies) or packaged in glass or aseptic cardboard containers, along with plastic container options next to them.

Choose the glass or cardboard container option when possible.

"Look for soups and sauces in aseptic cardboard containers, which are BPA-free."[81]

"Buy food in glass jars, which are BPA-free. Glass jars are easy to clean and can be reused for serving, drinking, storing, freezing, and heating foods."[82]

Some foods and drinks will be difficult to find in anything but plastic. It's important to keep in mind that we shoot for perfection, but, realistically, life isn't perfect and we don't always have access to the resources that we need in a way that we need them.

Sometimes we have access to food in bulk, glass, or cardboard containers but don't have the financial means to buy them or the time to prepare them. This is not an excuse to be used willy-nilly, but a strategy to be applied.

Dried toasted coconut flakes are a great example of this.

---

[81] '"Disrupted Development: The Dangers of Prenatal BPA Exposure," Breast Cancer Fund, September 2013: 12.
https://d124kohvtzl951.cloudfront.net/wp-content/uploads/2017/03/02025229/Report_Disrupted-Development-the-Dangers-of-Prenatal-BPA-Exposure_September_2013.pdf

[82] "Disrupted Development: The Dangers of Prenatal BPA Exposure," Breast Cancer Fund, September 2013: 12.
https://d124kohvtzl951.cloudfront.net/wp-content/uploads/2017/03/02025229/Report_Disrupted-Development-the-Dangers-of-Prenatal-BPA-Exposure_September_2013.pdf

The organic toasted coconut flakes that I buy are packaged in plastic. I could purchase an organic coconut whole, grate the coconut—break it out of the shell, grate the coconut, and toast it—and store it in a glass container. This process fulfills my priorities of eating organic and avoiding plastic packaging. But is it worth the investment of resources?

Making organic toasted coconut flakes is a very real possibility and is doable in general. For me, the time and scope of work involved in making my own toasted coconut flakes is time prohibitive. So I have included it on my list of things to work towards as I continue, alongside you, on my journey of living life with fewer chemicals one step at a time.

We, as individuals traveling similar paths to live life with fewer chemicals, each have to make the decision for ourselves as to what steps we can take right now to rid our homes of chemicals harming our health. Start by buying organic, then by minimizing or eliminating plastic packaging, and then turn your attention to buying local.

## Buy Local

How do you avoid exhaust and chemicals that food is exposed to during transportation? Quite simply, buy local.

Buying food from local sources helps to lessen chemicals found in food and to keep the food fresh naturally, without adding chemical preservatives.

It is important to understand that buying local and buying organic is not the same thing. Many people confuse these two distinctly different categories, and think that buying local inherently means the food is organic. Organic food is food that does not contain chemicals. Fresh food is food that is freshly picked or harvested. Each have their own health benefits. Ideally, food would be organic AND fresh!

It's hard for some people to think that their local farmer is selling food sprayed with pesticide and other chemicals. As my high school teacher, Mr. Brill, used to explain, people sometimes have a not-in-my-backyard mindset. For example, they know that chemicals can be found in food, but not in *my* backyard—not from my local farmer, not from my local community, not from my local farmer's market. That's simply not the case.

Every farmer is someone's local farmer. And they're spraying pesticides and chemicals onto crops just like they are in "other" communities.

When you buy local, be sure you're still buying organic. Ask local farmers if they spray their fields with pesticides or fertilizers or any type of chemicals. Ask if they have organic crops, and if so, are they certified USDA Organic crops?

Local farmer's market vendors typically do not package food. The whole point of a farmer's market is to make fresh food available to the local community, food that is freshly harvested.

The food is not sitting in plastics for a very long time—you buy it, put it in a bag (sometimes plastic), take it home, and take it out of the package. That food does not sit in plastic bags, on foam plates wrapped in plastic wrap. It comes unpackaged and ready for you to stuff into your own bag during the duration of your time at the farmer's market.

When the farmer's market food IS packaged, it's usually in the form of glass canning jars that contain things like jelly or pickled foods.

Food transportation time is drastically shortened from an average of nearly fifteen hundred miles to sixty miles or less, often times. Transportation chemicals can be largely avoided.

The bottom line is this: local farmers that have certified USDA Organic products + freshly harvested + unpackaged and sold in the local community = jackpot.

## Bag it in Cotton
Bring your own bag to pack your food in, particularly if it's unpackaged food. When you bring your own bag, make sure it's a cotton bag or made from fabric that does not contain chemicals.

Many of the bags (totes) that businesses give away to market their company are made of synthetic materials such a polypropylene which is a plastic. These bags or totes can release chemicals into the air and into your food. In addition these bags are typically not washable. Gross.

## Shop at Health Conscious Stores
We consumers can't control what products stores sell or what cleaners they choose to use. But we can control which stores we buy our groceries from.

Choose to shop at stores that are more solely focused on health consciousness.

There are organic grocery stores popping up and expanding faster than ever. These stores are not marketed as organic stores, because they don't carry ONLY organic. They do largely carry organic products—products with the USDA Organic seal and products that are partly organic.

These types of stores are more conscious of people's health, selling healthier and organic foods produced by local farmers. Examples of stores in southeastern Wisconsin are Outpost and Good Harvest Market. While the company operations are very different with Outpost being a co-op and Good Harvest being privately owned, both companies focus on organic and fresh foods.

Some stores advertise as being healthier, but their definition of healthy does not take into account chemicals found in foods. Like anything in life, pay attention to what's actually occurring. Pay attention to the amount of organic products they actually carry. It'll be clear as to if their definition of healthy includes fewer chemicals in foods.

Companies that are focused on people's health often use cleaners that have fewer chemicals in them.

This is different from grocery stores that have some organic food in their stores; stores that have a small section of organic or a few organic products on the grocery shelves.

Now, I recognize that our budgets—yours and mine—are not a blank check to be written. The money tree has not grown in the back yard. Shopping at health-conscious stores doesn't have to break the bank, as you'll see.

If you're not ready to shop at health-conscious grocery stores, standard grocery stores and big box stores can give us everyday-Joes the option to buy organic for less. While the ultimate goal is to buy food at health-conscious stores and avoid the harmful chemicals altogether, we each have to start somewhere. When you're at a point in your journey that allows you do so, be a little more choosey and shop at health-conscious grocery stores.

## Strategies

Strategies help us achieve our goals. It's one thing to understand where chemicals are found and what actions to take. It's another thing to actually do it. The strategies outlined here can help turn the idea of living life with fewer chemicals into a reality.

### Full Cabinets

Keep your cabinets as they are.

This may fly in the face of some advice that is more of an empty-your-cabinets-and-clear-your-shelves method, but I have found this to be an important step in my own life-changing process and the process for others I've guided. I say this with the utmost respect for people that advise otherwise, some of which are referenced in this book.

Here's why: since chemicals are found in *so many products*, not just food, if you subscribe to the clear-the-shelves method, you'll have to clear your food, clothing, furniture, personal care products, etc. all at once.

I don't know about you, but for me personally, this wasn't an option. I didn't have the time to understand the entire topic of chemicals in our everyday products, and I certainly didn't have the budget to get rid of all of our food, cloth belongings at once.

In fact, I don't know anyone that has (or is willing to invest) the time, money, or sanity to do that. So please don't. This does not need to be an overwhelming process, so let's not make it into one.

Instead, take it one step at a time. This is a process very manageable for anybody that wants to incorporate organic eating into their lives. One step at a time = big changes over time.

## Onesey-Twosey

Replace your food slowly with healthy food that has less chemicals. During your next trip to the grocery store, buy one item that has the USDA Organic label. That's it. That's your entire goal for the week.

After deciding to eat organic, on my first trip to the grocery store I purchased one thing—just one thing—that had the USDA Organic seal on the package.

I purchased a type of food that I typically purchased. Soup. I looked for the USDA Organic seal and found a few different options for organic soup. I could hardly believe it was that easy. I didn't spend hours or even minutes pouring over ingredient labels or hemming and hawing over what was organic.

I simply looked at the three brands of soups that had the seal on it, decided on which sounded the yummiest, compared the costs, and made a decision. It's that easy.

√eek One goal—accomplished.

I left the grocery store super excited. Not because picking out one organic product was a huge deal—clearly it was not. But because it was a huge deal that I made the conscious decision to start living my life with organic, less chemical products and ACTUALLY DID IT!

We've all experienced missed goals and empty promises in life. We intend to do something and we don't do it. And then we avoid it. For a long time. Out of fear or the feeling of being overwhelmed.

When I left the store, my excitement was because I took action. Because it was a real, true start to change our eating to organic so that our food wasn't damaging our cells. That might sound dramatic, but really it's not. If you stop a minute and think about it, that's exactly what's happening. You wouldn't consciously hurt your kids or yourself or your spouse (even when they make us mad!), so stop doing it unconsciously.

Here's how you do it: Write on your grocery list, "Buy one organic item with the USDA Organic seal."

That's your cue to remember to buy something organic. That's your trigger to say this is what I'm doing this week. Period. End of story. It's on my list. It's what I'm getting. It's what I'm going to do.

When you're successful in the Week One goal, celebrate. Give yourself a "YESSSSS!!!!" out loud (maybe in the car though) and a smile.

Each week after, slowly increase the number of organic items that you buy. By slowly, I mean increase buying one USDA Organic seal item to two or three, whichever you're comfortable with. Write down that goal on your grocery list. Then increase to four or five. And so on.

Here's how you develop your buying strategy for the following week: when you reach for the foods that you typically buy, take 10 seconds and look for options with a USDA Organic seal. Make a note to buy that item in organic next week. Your strategy will start to unfold week by week, one step at a time.

After a few weeks, this process will become automatic, not just when purchasing food, but any item.

Once your onesey-twosey organic food becomes many, it'll make sense to shop at health-conscious grocery stores. When I made this change, I LOVED it! Everyone there was like me—trying to eat food with fewer chemicals that was fresh, organic, locally grown, and truly good for our bodies. I felt like I belonged right away, a feeling that was harder to find as I became more and more immersed in the less-chemical way of life. That's the beauty and problem with emerging lifestyles—it's hard to find "your group," but when you do, you know it and fit right in.

You could decide to start shopping at a health-conscious store straight out of the gate. There's certainly nothing wrong with that! Keep in mind that you don't have to have an entire cart of organic on the first day. Work up to it. And as you do, there are companies that will reward your patronage.

## Organic Food Discounts

Organic and fresh food can be more expensive than chemical-filled foods. It's one of the reasons manufacturers add chemicals—less expensive production (by increasing food production and decreasing food loss).[83] Thankfully, retailers like Thrive Market, Whole Foods, Outpost, and Good Harvest are making organic food more affordable for everyone.

Health-conscious companies sometimes have give-back programs where customers can receive either a gift certificate or credit applied to their customer account. In some cases, the company will allow you to donate your account credit to a non-profit organization as a gesture of good will.

Organic food companies, such as Organic Valley, will send coupons to customers that are enrolled in their emailing or social media list. Every dollar counts.

And then there are companies that offer discounted organic products every day. I'm talking about Whole Foods (recently acquired by Amazon) and Thrive Market.

Thrive Market (https://thrivemarket.com) offers healthier and organic products that are discounted between 25-50% on each item. Woohoo! Not all of their products are organic, but they make shopping for organic very easy. There is a sort feature that allows you to only view organic foods. In addition, the pictures of each product are large enough to see

---

[83] "Exposure to Chemicals in Food," BreastCancer.org, Accessed February 9, 2017.
http://www.breastcancer.org/risk/factors/food_chem

the packaging and easily see if the product has the USDA Organic seal.

Even better, it's sooo easy to order staple foods from Thrive Market. I've ordered foods like oatmeal, soups, spices, and other packaged items that we'd typically keep on hand and regularly eat. Instead of purchasing them at the local grocery store, I started buying staple foods through Thrive Market for a discounted price and with little effort.

In my household, we order from Thrive Market once per month in quantities that will last the full four weeks. For example, if we've historically eaten three jars of applesauce and five bags of oatmeal in a month, we will order those same quantities at the same time each month. That way, we save money on discounts AND meet the minimum order amount of $49.00 (at the time of this publication) to qualify for free shipping!

You can set up recurring orders and shopping lists on the Thrive Market website to make the experience that.much.easier. I love it.

There is a membership fee of $59.00 annually (at the time of this book) that, to my household, is well worth the cost. Last year we saved over $800.00 in grocery bills. I was skeptical of this, wondering if the original retail costs were inflated. Low and behold they were not. The local grocery stores carrying organic products with the same weight and size were more expensive, every time. It's kind of a no brainer.

Thrive Market posts the ingredient labels as well, which is HUGE for those of us with food allergies or on strict food diets/lifestyles such as no sugar diets.

## EWG Cheat Sheets

Who doesn't love a good cheat sheet? Especially one that is developed by one of the most well-known advocates for products with fewer chemicals—the Environmental Working Group (EWG).

Every year, the EWG reviews test results from the U.S. Department of Agriculture that show the chemical content of produce (fruits and veggies), and then they publish two lists—*Dirty Dozen* and *Clean 15*.[84]

They rank food based on how many or how few chemicals are found in the food. The two lists work hand in hand to help us consumers, especially those of us that are not able to buy 100% organic 100% of the time, to prioritize what fruits and veggies are most important to buy organic.

Foods on the *Dirty Dozen* list are foods to *buy as organic*. If they made the *Dirty Dozen*, they have more chemicals compared to other fruits and veggies.

Foods on the *Clean 15* list are foods with the least amount of chemicals in them compared to other fruits and veggies. If you have to limit buying organic fruits and vegetables, these foods are less of a concern and could be purchased in non-organic until your budget is able to include them.

That doesn't mean that you should buy organic of all 12 items on the *Dirty Dozen* list in one week. It means that if you're planning to buy a fruit or veggie, check to see if it's on

---

[84] "Executive Summary: EWG's 2017 Shopper's Guide to Pesticides in Produce," Environmental Working Group, Accessed January 12, 2018.
https://www.ewg.org/foodnews/summary.php#.Wlzv9KinHIU

the *Dirty Dozen* or *Clean 15* and then decide if you'll buy that product as organic or not. If you're going to eat organic, you might as well get the biggest bang for your buck.

While I don't advocate for eating non-organic food, I have lived through and understand the limitations that life sometimes gives us. That is why it's so important to take it one step at a time.

One more step along the path toward living life with fewer chemicals is a good one. You don't have to throw away your budget, or spend hours and hours poring over tons of books and chemical names. You can look at lists of 12 and 15 products and buy your fruits and veggies strategically.

**Save Time**
Buying fresh organic fruits and veggies creates two concerns for most people: time and money. We've talked about money and budgets quite a bit, so let's look at how to save time.

Realistically, people are busy working long hours, taking care of and spending time with family, volunteering, and running in 12 directions all week long. With people and families short on time, cooking fresh food has become a less popular option.

Understandable.

No worries, though. That doesn't mean that you can't eat organic. Healthy organic meals can be whipped up in 20 minutes or less, AND most of those 20 minutes can be spent doing something else while dinner is cooking.

Here's the secret: Buy frozen organic fruits and veggies.

Frozen organic fruits can be added to plain yogurt, oatmeal, or smoothie ingredients and blended for a quick easy snack in minutes.

Dinners made from pre-cooked meat (invest only one hour on a Saturday or Sunday afternoon to cook meat for the week) can be paired with frozen organic veggies cooked over medium heat for 15-20 minutes. For even faster cook times, let the frozen veggies partially thaw in the refrigerator the day you plan to cook them.

Be creative. Mix green beans, broccoli, spinach, and carrots. Splash with organic olive oil and season with salt, pepper, and paprika or turmeric. Top with pre-cooked grass-fed or organic chicken breast. Done! Easily add organic pasta or quinoa if you're looking for a grain.

Frozen food eliminates the need for food prep and largely cooks by itself needing only a few stirs now and then. What do you do with your extra time!?

**Bonus – Quality Time**
As a surprise bonus, cooking frozen organic food became a bonding time between me and my teenage son.

If you have a teenager, you may be thinking, "That would never happen in *my* house with *my* teenager." That's what I thought too.

I'm the mom that hasn't been cool for years. Nor do I strive to be. Over the years I have worked hard to become a trusted confidant and source of guidance that is available when my teenager is ready to talk.

Cooking together has become one of the means that has allowed us to spend quality time together every night (that we're both home) without feeling forced or awkward. We choose the meal together, create seasoning concoctions, and either ooohhh and ahhhh over the delicious combination or aaapthaa yuck over the not-so-great trials.

In between that is real conversation about our day, life direction (handling difficult issues, future aspirations, exciting progress), and upcoming schedules.

You could spend the time doing dishes, paying bills, or just enjoying good music while you cook. So many possibilities.

**Buy Fresh Premium Organic**
Like most things in life, food generally comes in good, better, and best varieties.

As you know, organic food is measured by the amount of chemicals in the product, not measured by freshness. But eating frozen or fresh fruits and veggies can help reduce the amount of chemicals in food.

"Look for fresh or frozen fruits and vegetables. Not only will you avoid BPA, you will also avoid the sugar and salt that often accompany canned produce."[85]

---

[85] "Disrupted Development: The Dangers of Prenatal BPA Exposure," Breast Cancer Fund, September 2013: 12. https://d124kohvtzl951.cloudfront.net/wp-content/uploads/2017/03/02025229/Report_Disrupted-Development-the-Dangers-of-Prenatal-BPA-Exposure_September_2013.pdf

The freshest frozen organic veggies are labeled "premium organic." Cascadian Farms is an example of a company offering premium organic frozen foods. Ask your local grocery store if they carry premium quality or the freshest organic food available.

When you're ready to take the step of cooking organic fresh veggies (non-frozen), dedicate three or four hours on a Saturday or Sunday afternoon to chopping and cooking several dishes at once. Involve the family to make it a family affair with less work for everyone.

Even better, don't think of it as work or something you HAVE to do. Think of it as something you WANT to do. Think of it as working towards a happier and healthier life with fewer chemicals. Cooking fresh organic food can be a fun activity that creates fond memories of time spent together.

If you're single, find a friend to join you! Split the cost, split the food, or keep it for yourself. Any way you slice it, it's low-cost entertainment.

One step closer to living life with fewer chemicals AND eating fresh!

## One.Step.At.A.Time.
Small steps over time can make a big change in your life. Take small action steps each week to steer away from chemical-filled foods and towards living a life with fewer chemicals. Below are actionable steps to take as you continue your journey to a healthier you. Start with whatever step works best for you at this time in your life.

Just Starting:
1. Write these words at the top of your grocery list: "Buy one organic item with the USDA Organic label."
2. Look for the USDA Organic label on packaged foods, eggs, and dairy products and buy those. Week One, buy one item with the USDA Organic label. Week Two, buy two or three items with the USDA Organic label. Continue to increase each week.
3. Buy fruits and veggies following the *Dirty Dozen* and *Clean 15* suggestions.
4. Buy frozen organic fruits and veggies if time is a concern.

Advanced:
1. Shop at online discount stores such as Thrive Market. Order organic staple foods once per month to get the benefits of organic, discounts, and free shipping.
2. Pack your groceries in cotton bags.
3. Buy organic fruits, veggies, nuts, and grains in bulk, not packaged. Caution to people with food allergies to avoid bulk food if it is near foods you are allergic to.
4. Buy organic food and beverages in glass jars or cardboard containers whenever possible. Skip the plastic containers.

Super Star:
1. Buy fresh premium organic to get the benefits of organic (95-100% organic) AND fresh food. This includes buying local from organic farmers, CSAs, and buying premium frozen produce.
2. Shop at health-conscious grocery stores that use cleaners with fewer chemicals.

3. Store organic, fresh food in glass containers. This topic will be covered more in Chapter 6 – Household Products.

# Chapter 5
# Clothing

Adam and Eve might have been on to something—using natural materials for clothing. It sits against our skin all day and night.

Clothing protects us from the wind, rain, and cold. It announces our style and sometimes our mood. It can make us feel important and confidant. It can make or break a job interview. It can signal a trip to the gym or indicate a profession. It gives us comfort when we're sick or tired.

From pants to pajamas, the type of material, dye, and finish can contain chemicals that may be causing health conditions.

In addition to clothing material, the number of clothes can have an impact on health. It sounds a little weird, but consider this:

According to the U.S. Bureau of Labor Statistics, in 2010 the average household spent an average of $1,700 per year on clothing, shoes, and related products.[86]

---

[86] "How Much Do Consumers Spend on Apparel?" U.S. Department of Labor, Bureau of Labor Statistics. Spotlight on Statistics: 2.

The average American woman owns 30 outfits, one for each day of the month. Back in 1930 that number was nine, one for each day of the week plus two extras.[87]

That's more than three times the number of outfits hanging in our closet today—well, at least 3+ times. That's per female.

The more clothing we have in our closets + more clothing made from chemicals (this is really happening) = more exposure to chemicals that have been linked to health conditions.

Where are these chemicals found?

**Materials**
Go to your closet and check your tags.

Count the number of shirts, pants, underwear, and bras that are made from polyester, nylon, rayon, spandex, vinyl, viscose, and acrylic. [88] Just one total for all seven types of material is fine. This category of materials is called synthetic materials.

Now count the number of clothes that are made of cotton, hemp, linen, and wool. One total for all four types of material works great. This category of materials is called natural materials.

Compare your two totals. Which category has the highest number?

---

https://www.bls.gov/spotlight/2012/fashion/
[87] Joshua Becker, "21 Surprising Statistics That Reveal How Much Stuff We Actually Own," becomingminimalist, Accessed March 23, 2017. https://www.becomingminimalist.com/clutter-stats/
[88] http://www.synthetictextiles.org/

My closet used to have a 95/5 ratio—95% synthetic materials and 5% natural materials. Most people would say their closets and drawers were primarily filled with synthetics.

Synthetic materials are made out of man-made chemicals, specifically they are oil byproducts. The Petroleum Services of Canada even has a short video showing a few types of clothing made from oil and gas products.[89]

It's the same material that plastics are made of. In fact, when synthetic clothing starts on fire it melts.[90] Yes, melts. Crazy!

About two years ago, a mainstream store was selling polyester sweatshirts made from 25% recycled plastic. On the one hand, recycling is good for our environment, which is a win for all of us. On the other hand, it's still clothing made of plastic which is not good for people.

The American Chemical Society sums it up well in their overview of synthetic textiles. The opening statement is this: "Ever wonder how certain fabrics protect against the bitter cold, keep athletes cool, or stretch with you as you bend? It's all textile chemistry!"[91]

Plastic and oil byproducts, including synthetic materials used to make clothing, have been identified as harmful to

---

[89] Petroleum Services Association of Canada. "Clothing," Facts about Canada's Oil and Natural Gas Industry, Accessed March 26, 2017.
https://oilandgasinfo.ca/products/clothing/
[90] City of Phoenix, "Flammable Fabrics," Accessed November 23, 2017.
https://www.phoenix.gov/fire/safety-information/home/fabrics
[91] American Chemical, "Textile Chemistry," Overview, Accessed November 23, 2017.
https://www.acs.org/content/acs/en/careers/college-to-career/chemistry-careers/textile-chemistry.html

people's health by experts in the science and health professions.[92]

Sweatshirts or other clothing made from synthetic material, even recycled plastic bottles, may not be healthy for people. I love the idea of recycling products... when those products are not harmful to people. Creating and recycling products with chemicals that are harming us in the first place seems like a circular exposure of chemicals that is unnecessary. Perhaps we could simply stop using them in the first place.

## Finishes

New clothing contains finishes, made from chemicals. I'd say it comes free of charge! But it doesn't. The retail price does include the cost of adding chemical finishes to clothing.

Clothing manufactures may use different amounts and types of chemicals as finishes.

No iron, wrinkle-free, waterproof. These are a few types of clothing on the market today that contain chemicals that may be harmful to people's health. The finishes are typically achieved by adding chemicals to the top of materials.

To illustrate this idea, think of staining wood. The wood is stained and a clear coat finish is put over it to seal the wood. With clothing, the cloth is dyed with color and then finishes are added to the surface of the materials to make the materials wrinkle-free, no iron, appear smooth, or give them a sheen.

---

[92] Ecology Center, "Adverse Health Effects of Plastics," Accessed November 20, 2017.
https://ecologycenter.org/factsheets/adverse-health-effects-of-plastics/

Smooth finishes can also be achieved by weaving the thread a certain way during the manufacturing of the material. It's difficult for us common folk consumers to tell which finishes are made of chemicals and which are created from the weave style.

### Dyes & Bleaches

In addition to synthetic materials being derived from oil, so go the dyes in clothing.[93] Dyes can be made from oil byproducts and synthetics, which by definition are "compounds formed through a chemical process by human agency, as opposed to those of natural origin."[94]

When dying clothing, two factors are taken into consideration: the material type (synthetic or natural), and dye type (chemical-based or natural). Certain materials absorb dyes easier, and specific dyes can only be effectively used on specific materials.[95]

Polyester, acrylic, nylon and other synthetic materials do not absorb natural dyes; they require chemical-based dyes be

---

[93] Brendan Borrell, "Where does blue food dye come from?" Scientific American, January 2009.
https://www.scientificamerican.com/article/where-does-blue-food-dye/
[94] Dictionary.com, "Synthetic."
http://www.dictionary.com/browse/synthetic?s=t
[95] Science Buddies, "Staining Science: Make the Boldest, Brightest Dye!" A colorful challenge from Science Buddies. Scientific American. January 2009.
https://www.scientificamerican.com/article/bring-science-home-brightest-dye/

used.[96] Natural materials absorb natural dyes and chemical-based dyes easier than synthetic materials.[97]

Let's look at this more succinctly.

Synthetic clothes + chemical-based dyes = chemicals in both material and dye

Natural clothes + chemical-based dyes = chemicals in only dye

Natural clothes + natural dyes = no chemicals in material or dye

Vivid and dark-colored materials require more dye be added to the material. For darker colors, the dyer mixes several dyes together to get the right shade.[98] Black shirts may have more dyes than yellow shirts and bright yellow shirts may have more dye than pastel yellow shirts.

White clothing typically doesn't start out as white materials. Cotton, for example, is naturally a light yellow-brown color. In order to produce white cotton clothing, the material is bleached. Often times, bleach or chlorine is used to whiten clothing.

---

[96] Science Buddies, "Staining Science: Make the Boldest, Brightest Dye!" A colorful challenge from Science Buddies. Scientific American. January 2009. https://www.scientificamerican.com/article/bring-science-home-brightest-dye/

[97] Science Buddies, "Staining Science: Make the Boldest, Brightest Dye!" A colorful challenge from Science Buddies. Scientific American. January 2009. https://www.scientificamerican.com/article/bring-science-home-brightest-dye/

[98] The Essential Chemical Industry – online, "Colorants," Date last amended March 18, 2013. http://essentialchemicalindustry.org/materials-and-applications/colorants.html

## Washing clothing

Believe it or not, the way you wash clothes can make a difference in the amount of chemicals you're exposed to all day long.[99]

The way soap works is this: soap suds grab dirt and chemicals on clothes and pull them away from the fabric. When too much soap is used, the suds may not fully rinse clean and can get stuck in areas like under a collar on a shirt.[100]

Overfilling the washing machine can also result in un-cleaned clothing. In order to wash clothes properly, the clothes need space to move. If the machine is overfilled, not all clothes will be cleaned.[101]

Washing with warm water shrinks clothing, but activates chemicals.[102] We'll get into the details of this soon.

---

[99] Public Broadcasting Station, "How You Should Be Doing Laundry" You're Doing it Wrong. Television show. Performed by Randy and Jason. Aired 12/31/15. Public Broadcasting Station. 2015.
http://www.pbs.org/video/youre-doing-it-wrong-how-you-should-be-doing-laundry/

[100] Public Broadcasting Station, "How You Should Be Doing Laundry," You're Doing it Wrong. Television show. Performed by Randy and Jason. Aired 12/31/15. Public Broadcasting Station. 2015.
http://www.pbs.org/video/youre-doing-it-wrong-how-you-should-be-doing-laundry/

[101] Public Broadcasting Station, "How You Should Be Doing Laundry," You're Doing it Wrong. Television show. Performed by Randy and Jason. Aired 12/31/15. Public Broadcasting Station. 2015.
http://www.pbs.org/video/youre-doing-it-wrong-how-you-should-be-doing-laundry/

[102] Emily Sennebogen, "Do clothes always shrink if you wash in warm water?" How Stuff Works, April 13, 2012.
https://home.howstuffworks.com/home-improvement/household-hints-tips/cleaning-organizing/do-clothes-always-shrink-if-you-wash-in-warm-water.htm

Washing clothes properly could help rid of chemical finishes and residual dyes quicker.

**Designs & Decals**

Shirts, particularly t-shirts and sweatshirts, often come designed with logos and graphics on the front and back. The logos and graphics can be created by screen printing, embroidery, or adhering vinyl or plastic decals.

Screen printing is achieved by adding different dye colors to the material to create the pattern desired. Shirts can arrive at the screen printing facility in white or already dyed. During screen printing, another color is added to create lettering or an image.

Often time ink dyes are oil-based as described above, but can be any of the dye types that we've already discussed.

Embroidery is stitching designs, often times logos, into a shirt. The entire design is made from thread. Embroidery does typically include a material called interfacing on the back of the design that, over time, can fall off or break down, depending on how large the image is and the type of interfacing used.

Interfacing is often times made from polyester. Some interfacing, on larger images remains intact throughout the life of the shirt. Interfacing is also used around buttonholes and in collars.

Vinyl designs or lettering on shirts have vinyl or plastic adhered right to the shirt itself. Vinyl has been repeatedly identified by scientists and medical professionals as one of the most harmful materials to people's health.

Vinyl, at normal room temperatures, off-gases chemicals that are harming our health. Heated vinyl, such as those heated during the clothes drying process, off-gases even more chemicals. Stay away from vinyl if you can.

Another type of clothing decal is sequins or fake stones added to clothing. I call this bling.

Sequins are made from a flimsy flexible plastic. If you've tried to sew sequins onto material, you know that the small buggers easily drop from your fingers if you don't hold them just right. Similar to heated vinyl, heated plastic sequins (or any heated plastic) off-gases chemicals at a more intense rate than cold or room temperature plastic.

Similarly, fake stones are made of plastic despite best efforts to make they look like actual stones. These are seen on women's shirts and jean pockets. Often times the blinged-out clothing is for professional offices or dressier occasions, but sometimes women in their 30s and 40s can be seen sporting rhinestone jeans and cowboy boots at the local high school football games. Yeehaaw!

## Packaging

Packaged clothing, if ordered online, comes wrapped in plastic. Plastic from the packaging off-gases into the air and into the clothing material itself, and remains there until washed out.[103]

---

[103] "Indoor Air Quality," Scientific Findings Resource Bank, Berkley Lab, Accessed January 12, 2018.
https://iaqscience.lbl.gov/voc-svocs

## Soaps, Softeners, & Fragrances

Have you ever had a skin irritation or condition like psoriasis or eczema and gone to the dermatologist? One of the first questions they ask is what you use for soaps and softeners. And for good reason.

Laundry soaps, dryer sheets, and liquid softeners contain chemicals that can be highly irritating to the skin, and may be affecting our health in many different ways.[104] [105]

Soaps and softeners leave a residue on clothing, bedding, and towels that is absorbed by the skin and inhaled throughout the days and nights.[106] You can actually feel this residue. It is the reason clothes feel a little softer—it's the layer of chemicals on top of the fabric.[107]

Standard dryer sheets are made from polyester, a material made from oil byproduct that may be affecting health.[108]

---

[104] Alex Scranton, "Ditch the Dryer Sheets!," Women's Voices for the Earth, April 4, 2013.
https://www.womensvoices.org/2013/04/04/ditch-the-dryer-sheets/

[105] Megan Boyle, Samara Geller, "Skip the Fabric Softeners," Environmental Working Group, May 5, 2016.
https://www.ewg.org/enviroblog/2016/05/skip-fabric-softeners#.WlmQ0qinHIV

[106] Maia James, "Safe Laundry Detergent Guide," Gimme the Good Stuff, January 20, 2013.
https://gimmethegoodstuff.org/safe-product-guides/laundry-detergent/

[107] Rebecca Sutton, "Don't get slimed: Skip the fabric softener," Environmental Working Group, News and Analysis, November 1, 2011.
https://www.ewg.org/enviroblog/2011/11/dont-get-slimed-skip-fabric-softener#.WlmSe6inHIV

[108] Chris Morrisson, "How Dryer Sheets Work," How Stuff Works, November 30, 2009.
https://home.howstuffworks.com/dryer-sheets2.htm

In addition to chemicals, dryer sheets contain wax. If you think of the dryer process, it heats clothes and anything else in the dryer. What does wax do when it heats? It gets soft. And when it gets soft, it sticks to everything, including your clothing and the dryer itself.

Wax from dryer sheets heats up and sticks to the dryer drum, building up over time.

Laundromats are a great example of seeing leftover wax in action. When you throw your clothes into a dryer that previously had dryer sheets, you can still smell the dryer sheets. You can feel the wax in the drum if you run your fingers over the metal.

Of course, timing matters too. If dryer sheets were used right before you arrived, it's more likely that you can still feel and smell the dryer sheets versus if it was a couple of people ago.

Wax, as we all know, is water resistant making it even more difficult to wash chemicals and fragrances from clothing.

That brings us to scented or fragranced soaps and softeners that contain extra chemicals.

All it takes is a stroll down the laundry detergent aisle to realize just how many soaps and softeners have scent added to them. The waft of scents (and chemicals) can be overpowering.

Those fragrances, or scents, are manufactured from a mix of chemicals. The number of chemicals needed to make synthetic fragrances may be in the hundreds.[109] When fragrances are added to soaps and softeners, here's what happens.

You have potentially hundreds of chemicals in a scent + chemicals in the soap or softener itself = hundreds of chemicals that may be causing the health issues that were mentioned in Chapter 2.

Another way fragrances can be added to clothing is by spraying the fragrance on. I'm talking about colognes, body sprays, and perfumes. These fragrances get absorbed into clothing.

Think about your own experience. If you put on perfume, body spray, or cologne in the morning before work, then at the end of the day throw your clothing in the laundry hamper, three days later you can go into the laundry hamper and still smell the fragrance you put on three days ago. That's no coincidence. The fragrance has absorbed into the clothing. Over time, that fragrance becomes difficult and sometimes impossible to remove.

Fragrance doesn't discriminate. Various types of clothing material—polyester, nylon, cotton, organic cotton, wool, etc.—will absorb the fragrance chemicals and hold on to them over time.

---

[109] Rebecca Sutton, "Don't get slimed: Skip the fabric softener," Environmental Working Group, News and Analysis, November 1, 2011. https://www.ewg.org/enviroblog/2011/11/dont-get-slimed-skip-fabric-softener#.WlmSe6inHlV

### Solutions!
**Material**

Flip the 95/5 to 5/95 by purchasing 95%-100% of your clothing made from natural materials.

Natural materials are made from nature-made materials. Nature-made materials can have chemicals added to them during processing, but if left in their virgin state, they are not harmful to people's health. Types of natural materials include cotton, linen, silk, hemp, and wool.[110]

Within the cotton family there are various types of cotton that fall into one of two categories: American upland which is a short-staple cotton or American pima which is an extra-long staple cotton. Short-staple cotton is standard in the U.S. and accounts for 97% of U.S. cotton production.[111] While cotton is a healthy product in and of itself, it is heavily treated with pesticides. In fact, pesticides sprayed on cotton total 16% of total pesticides uses in the world, even though cotton crops only cover 2.5% of cultivated land.[112]

Extra-long staple cotton includes pima cotton, Supima cotton (indicating 100% pima cotton products), and some Egyptian cotton. Extra-long staple cotton has two qualities that can help minimize the amount of chemicals added to the material: 1) the finished product can have a smooth feeling

---

[110] Kate Fletcher, "Natural Textiles," Sustainable Design Award. 1999. http://www.sda-uk.org/materials/textiles/natural_textiles.htm

[111] Agricultural Marketing Resource Center, "Cotton," Profile revised September 2017. https://www.agmrc.org/commodities-products/fiber/cotton/

[112] Rodale Institute, "Chemical cotton," Dig Deeper, February 4, 2014. https://rodaleinstitute.org/chemical-cotton/

without using chemicals in the finish process to make it feel smooth, and 2) the cotton is durable.[113]

Clothing can be a blend of materials as well, such as 60% cotton and 40% polyester. Or a blend of short-strand cotton and extra-long strand cotton. There are many blends used in the clothing industry, but it all boils down to the same basic principles that we've covered. Natural materials have the least amount of chemicals (and maybe none at all).

The mac-daddy of materials comes in organic varieties. Organic cottons, linen, and wool. Typically, they're labeled as organic. Organic materials are grown free of pesticides and other chemicals that are harmful to people's health.

Here's the kicker, though. Just because clothing is made from organic materials does not mean it's free of chemicals. It solely means that the material was grown free of pesticides and other chemicals. What happens after that point can be an entirely different story.

**Finishes**

When clothing labels say no iron, wrinkle-free, permanent press, and waterproof, leave it on the rack—both in the literal sense and virtual shopping sense. Beyond these well known finishes, manufacturers could add chemical finishes and not advertise it. It would be great if manufactures would list the chemicals added to their clothing, but, just like the food industry, they don't.

---

[113] Kurt Nolte, "Pima cotton," Yuma County Cooperative Extension. https://cals.arizona.edu/fps/sites/cals.arizona.edu.fps/files/cotw/Pima_Cotton.pdf

A few tell-tale signs of chemicals in clothing can be determined if you:

- Smell it. If the material smells like chemicals, it very likely has chemicals. Avoid it. It's important to note that many chemicals do not have a smell to them, so depending entirely on smell is not a fool-proof method. It's simply one of the oh-my-gosh moments that might cause you to wonder if chemicals were added.
- Feel it. Sometimes materials feel stiff or scratchy. If you don't feel good wearing it, then don't.

Of course, if you're ordering online you can't smell or feel the clothing until you receive it. In this case, read the online product descriptions to try to determine if there are chemicals. I'll be honest. Finishes can be one of the trickiest things to avoid in clothing (and other textiles).

No worries, though. Credible third-party certifying organizations dedicated to looking out for consumer health can help! For free! We'll get to that soon.

**Dyes & Bleaches**

Clothing labels don't typically advertise the type of dye used in clothing, but some online stores do list the dye used—particularly if they consider it to be a dye that has fewer chemicals—as a marketing statement.

Low-impact dyes have become popular, and there is some controversy over if they are healthier or not. Materials that are colored with low-impact dyes mean that less dye is needed to color the material. The dyes are made with chemicals that cause them to absorb and adhere to the material quicker.[114] Low-impact dyes are still made from chemicals though, making them a synthetic dye.[115]

Natural dyes are made from natural products, such as clay, tree bark, plants, berries, minerals, and seeds.[116] This is how clothing was died in the early days, before chemical-based dyes were used.

Natural whitening agents, such as hydrogen peroxide, are used by some manufacturers as a way to whiten clothing using healthier ingredients.

## Washing Clothing

This one's a no brainer and sooo easy to do. If you're not washing your clothes correctly, you're not washing out the dirt and chemicals that we come in contact with every day. Before you dismiss this statement by thinking, "I don't work with chemicals so it doesn't apply to me," consider this:

If you clean kitchen counters with chemical solution, have your hair cut in a beauty shop, go shopping, buy any of the many thousands of items that are off-gassing chemicals, or head to the hardware store full of fresh fertilizer bags, then your clothing may have chemicals absorbed into them.[117]

---

[114] Coyuchi, "Why use low-impact dyes?" August 8, 2017. https://www.coyuchi.com/the-naturalista/lowimpactdyes/
[115] Organic Lifestyle, "Fibre Reactive / Low Impact dyes." https://organiclifestyle.com/articles/fibre-reactive-low-impact-dyes?currency_code=USD
[116] Lowimpact.org, "Natural dyes: introduction." https://www.lowimpact.org/lowimpact-topic/natural-dyes/
[117] "Indoor Air Quality," Scientific Findings Resource Bank, Berkley Lab, Accessed January 12, 2018. https://iaqscience.lbl.gov/voc-svocs

If you're buying new clothes, they come with chemicals. Used clothes too.

How do you wash your clothes to get them fully cleaned?

It starts when you add the soap. Before you add clothes to the washing machine, pour the soap (liquid or powder) into the bottom of the washing machine (if you don't have a detergent dispenser in your washing machine). Fill the washer with three to four inches of water.

Add clothes so that the washer is half to three-quarters full. Don't push the laundry down; leave it loose and fluffy. When the washer is overfilled, the clothes can't move around enough to get clean.

To understand this better, think of a time you were gardening without gloves. After planting flowers your hands were dirt-caked. If you were to wash your hands with soap inside of a glass cup, you would have very restricted movement between your hands and the soap. Your hands would have dirt remaining on them. Whereas if you washed your hands with soap in the sink and had unlimited movement, your hands would be fully cleaned.

The same thing happens with clothing.

Before clothes are washed, there is dirt, pollen, food, chemicals, etc., on the clothing. When clothing is mashed into the washer and has restricted room to wash, the clothing may not be fully cleaned.

During the rinse cycle (or in the rinse dispenser) add vinegar—yes vinegar!—as your clothing softener.

For clothes that have higher amounts of chemicals, such as new clothes or stubborn fragrances, wash them in hot water to activate soap chemicals and the chemicals in the clothing in an attempt to clean the clothes quicker.

## Designs and Decals

Designs that are added to clothing using natural dyes are a healthier option. Patterns added right into the material such as checkered or gingham patterns, ink lettering, and screen printed graphics can be a great way to add interest to your clothing without added chemicals—as long as the dyes used are natural dyes.

While embroidery thread and interfacing can be made from polyester, the amount of polyester in embroidered shirts is small compared to an entire shirt made from synthetic material. Given that, embroidery may be a better option in the way of shirt designs.

Steer away from vinyl and plastic designs and decals on clothing to avoid chemicals in plastics, vinyl, and the additional off-gassing that occurs in any temperature but intensifies during the drying process when these materials heat up. This includes avoiding sequins or fake stones made from plastic.

Of course, there is nothing wrong with plain clothes too! Layer different colors and styles of clothing to create outfits that look professional, casual, and classy.

## Packaging

Similar to health-conscious grocery stores, there are health conscious clothing stores that sell all-organic or mostly-organic products.

Health-conscious organic clothing companies typically wrap their clothing in paper tissue or cardboard box versus plastic. In fact, in order to become a Global Organic Textile Standard (GOTS) Organic certified product, the product must not have plastic in the packaging (or tags for that matter).[118]

As you start buying clothing with less chemicals, you will, just by nature of the company you're purchasing from, start buying clothes that are wrapped in tissue, not wrapped in plastic.

Plastic avoided. Count it as a win!

## Soaps, Softeners, & Fragrances

One of the easiest steps to take is to avoid fragranced or scented laundry soaps and fabric softeners.

There are products that are "unscented" and often advertised of being "free" of scents or "clear" of dyes (oh, yeah, soaps can also contain dyes that are not good for people's health).

But even non-scented products can contain chemicals.

"Unscented" products may still contain fragrance-chemicals that are meant to mask the smell of other chemicals or

---

[118] http://www.global-standard.org/

materials. "Fragrance free" products are typically free of fragrance-chemicals.[119]

Bottom line is that "fragrance free" products give the best opportunity for us consumers to actually have a no-fragrance-chemical product.[120]

Just to be clear, if you have a fragrance free product, that doesn't mean there are no chemicals in it. It simply means that the fragrance chemicals aren't in it.

Lucky for us everyday consumers, the Environmental Working Group (ewg.org) publishes a database of cleaning products that have been tested and rated for health hazards. Laundry detergents fall into that category.

The beauty of the EWG database is that is makes it so easy to find laundry soaps that have fewer harmful chemicals in them. Some of the soaps rated as "A" or "B" can be found at the local grocery store or health-conscious grocery stores.

White vinegar can be used as a fabric softener and rinsing agent. In fact, it's super helpful in getting rid of body odor and musty smells in clothing.[121] Armpit smells that are stuck in shirts disappear.

Vinegar takes care of these smells for two reasons—it's an antibacterial agent, so it kills the bacteria that is causing the

---

[119] Sophia Ruan Gushee, *A to Z of D-Toxing: The Ultimate Guide to Reducing Our Toxic Exposures.* (New York: The S File Publishing, LLC, 2015), 151.

[120] Sophia Ruan Gushee, *A to Z of D-Toxing: The Ultimate Guide to Reducing Our Toxic Exposures.* (New York: The S File Publishing, LLC, 2015), 151.

[121] Christine Halvorson, "Uses for Vinegar: Doing Laundry." https://home.howstuffworks.com/home-improvement/household-hints-tips/cleaning-organizing/uses-for-vinegar-doing-laundry-ga.htm

B.O. and mustiness, and freshens the laundry. Vinegar is also used to remove stains, wash out chemicals from new clothing, reduce static,[122] and dissolve hard water scale.[123]

For many decades people have been using white vinegar with no adverse health effects. The EWG gives white vinegar an "A" rating, indicating the healthiest score a product can have.

Even better, white vinegar is less expensive than most fabric softeners. And, it can be found in nearly any grocery store, making it easily accessible to all. Double bonus!

## Strategies

In order to actually DO, it's helpful to have a strategy—a shortcut, so to speak—for how to easily take steps to living life with fewer chemicals.

## GOTS

GOTS is not improper English use. It stands for Global Organic Textile Standard (GOTS).

Get to know and love GOTS. They are the world leader in setting standards for processing textiles made from organic fibers. [124] They certify products that have fewer chemicals in fiber production (farming) and manufacturing.

---

[122] Christine Halvorson, "Uses for Vinegar: Doing Laundry." https://home.howstuffworks.com/home-improvement/household-hints-tips/cleaning-organizing/uses-for-vinegar-doing-laundry-ga.htm

[123] Healthy Child Healthy World. "4 Nontoxic Cleaners That Should be in Every Home." http://www.healthychild.org/4-nontoxic-cleaners-that-should-be-in-every-home/

[124] "The Standard," Global Organic Textile Standard, Ecology & Social Responsibility, Last Updated May 23, 2017. http://www.global-standard.org/the-standard.html

GOTS has two levels of certification:

### 1. GOTS Organic – 95% to 100% Organic

GOTS certification that says "organic" means that the material is made with 95% or more of organic fibers. Look for the GOTS label that looks similar to this:

It means that the product with the GOTS label stating "organic" contains a minimum of 95% certified organic fibers.

### 2. GOTS Made with Organic

GOTS labels that state "made with organic" mean the material is made with 70% or more of certified organic fibers.[125]

Products with less than 70% organic fibers are not certified by GOTS.

When considering products for certification, GOTS considers the types and amounts of chemicals added such as dyes and finishes. Certain chemicals are prohibited completely, as are genetically modified organisms (GMOs). Accessory material is also considered and has restrictions on textile materials

---

[125] "General Description," Global Organic Textile Standard, Ecology & Social Responsibility, Last Updated May 23, 2017.
http://www.global-standard.org/the-standard.html

such as PVC (a type of plastic) along with packaging materials which must be made of paper or cardboard.

The GOTS requires that material fiber producers and manufacturers follow specific guidelines when it comes to the environment and social responsibility as well. The organization is worthwhile to read about.[126]

Look for the GOTS Organic label as an easy way to identify clothing that contains fewer chemicals.

### Scan Tags

A quick scan of a clothing tag can tell you what the material is made from, what its care instructions are, and sometimes the finishes on a product (e.g., no iron, wrinkle-free). If a tag does not have a finish listed, that does not mean it is free of finish chemicals. It simply means that the finish is not being marketed to consumers.

Online shopping may provide more detailed product information. Look through the product description details and care instructions. It only takes a few seconds to read through each tab of the product description and find key words like organic cotton, low impact dye, wrinkle-free, or no iron to know if it's a product you want to purchase. This is also the spot to look for GOTS certification logos.

The trick with online shopping is that sometimes the information is falsely stated, starting with the search results.

On some retail clothing websites, typing "100% organic cotton" or "100% pima cotton" into the search bar results in

---

[126] http://www.global-standard.org/

clothing that contains *some* cotton such as 40% cotton/60% polyester, or results with 100% of *any fabric* such as 100% polyester. The search feature is only picking the "100%" and not the full "100% cotton," even when the words are between quotations.

Be sure to click on the actual product description for each item to make sure that the search results are truly what you were looking for.

Product descriptions can also be falsely stated. At times the company will state "organic cotton" in the product name but list "cotton" in the product description. Inconsistencies in descriptions are an indication that you have a 50/50 chance of receiving organic cotton and 50/50 chance of receiving cotton.

## Dry Clean Only

Fabrics that are dry clean only, I'd advise steering clear of. Sometimes dry clean clothes you can hand wash or machine wash on a delicate cycle and hang dry; however, that's not always the case.

If there is a piece of clothing that you absolutely must have and it's truly dry clean only, then look into using a natural dry cleaning company. Dry cleaning itself uses chemicals to clean clothing. Natural dry cleaners use chemicals too, but different chemicals that are supposed to be nontoxic according to Green America.[127]

I'm still an advocate for skipping dry clean only clothing myself. But if that approach doesn't work for you, choose a

---

[127] "Green Dry Cleaning," Green America. Accessed February 27, 2017. https://www.greenamerica.org/green-living/green-dry-cleaning

natural dry cleaner. The idea here is to take steps to living a life with fewer chemicals.

## New vs. Used Clothes

Like anything in life, there are pros and cons to each of the choices we're faced with everyday. Clothing is no different, coming with its own set of pros and cons when deciding between buying new clothing and buying used clothing.

The "right" answer is an individual decision based on factors such as budget, time, health goal, and existing sensitivities and medical conditions. Let's look at the pros and cons for each option.

### New Clothing – Pros

New clothes have not been washed with or dried in soaps and softeners with chemicals or fragrances. They are free of other peoples' laundry detergents and fabric softeners.

The beauty of this scenario is that if you choose to use soaps and softeners that do not have fragrances or chemicals in them, your clothes will have fewer chemicals typically added during the wash and dry cycles.

Unworn clothing could have fewer fragrances from perfumes, colognes, body sprays, and body lotions.

I say *could*, because many brick-and-mortar retail stores today have air fresheners that spray a fine mist of scent into the air and into clothing. The scent, similar to personal fragrances, is absorbed by clothing (and other porous products).

New Clothing – Cons

New clothing comes with the finishes freshly applied and fully intact.

Depending on the amount and type of finishes that were added during manufacturing, it can take anywhere between a few washes to a zillion washes for the chemicals to wash out of new clothes. Some clothing, even after a zillion washes, will still have finishes adhering tightly to the material.

New clothing comes with fresh dyes as well. In some cases, the residual dyes have not been washed out of new clothes, or the dyes can release throughout the life of the clothing with the most dyes being released during the first few washes.

Take blue jeans, for example. When you wash a new pair of blue jeans, watch the discharge water from the washing machine (that discharges into your utility tub) for the first few washes. The water is distinctively blue. Super duper blue.

The dyes and manufacturing fibers left behind during processing are coming off in the wash, turning the water blue. Even after washing the jeans 2, 3, 4+ times, sometimes you can still see the dyes running through the discharge water into the utility tub.

I've seen this happen with brown denim jackets as well.

It's a great example of what happens with dye and other chemicals in new clothing, and how it can take several washes for the excess dyes in clothing to wash out.

At the end of this excess-dye-removal process, the jeans are still blue, of course, indicating that there is plenty of dye still remaining that has been absorbed by the material. But the point here is that dyes sometimes need to be washed from new clothes.

## Used Clothing – Pros
Used clothing is less expensive.

When I started converting my wardrobe from polyester and nylon to cottons, I started shopping at some of the local thrift stores. I would go purchase a cart full of clothes that were made of natural products, mostly cotton since it was easiest to find. Sometimes I struck it lucky and would find a piece of 100% organic cotton clothing.

It was easier to find clothes for me than it was for my grade-school-aged son. But hey, at least it was a step. It was an affordable way for me to convert my closet with a relatively small upfront cost.

Finishes and dyes that were originally put into the clothes have largely been worn (washed) off by the time you buy (or receive) used clothing.

## Used Clothing – Cons
Used clothes can have worn tags that make it difficult to read the material composition.

Used clothing has been washed by others that could have used fragranced soaps and fabric softeners that may be stuck in clothing. Or it may have been sprayed with perfumes, colognes, and body sprays that have become stuck in clothing material.

Chemicals and fragrances that were absorbed or imbedded into the clothing from people before you may be difficult to get out.

In my experience, women's tops were the toughest, particularly dress shirts. They seemed to contain the most fragrance and smelled like perfume, even after more than 25 washings. At times, I've re-donated, recycled, or thrown away clothing when I couldn't get the fragrance out of them.

These moments were frustrating, but then again, the topic of chemicals in our clothing and everyday products is somewhat frustrating as well—so perhaps it's just par for the course.

Choosing between new and used clothing is a matter of what type of challenge you'd like to face and what your current resources will allow for.

The goal here is to take steps to be exposed to fewer chemicals in our everyday products. Wearing cotton clothing with fragrances may be better than wearing polyester clothing with fragrances, strictly in the spirit of taking steps toward living life with fewer chemicals.

Even if it's not your ultimate goal, it's still a step that counts in a big way. It's all about small steps and taking a step in the right direction.

## Pre-Washing Off-Site

Clothing, new or used, coming into the home can stink up the house with unwanted chemicals. In addition, new clothing has "manufacturing dust" (I call it) which are the little fuzzies left behind from manufacturing the clothing. New clothes, even those certified by GOTS, should be washed before being worn to remove the manufacturing dust and any light chemicals that might be on the clothes.

Take the new or new-to-you (used) clothing to the laundromat for the first initial wash. Wipe out the washer before loading your clothes to remove soap residue left behind that may have chemicals or fragrances in it. Wash the clothes. After the first cycle, wash them again. Yep, start 'em right back up. Use soap that has zero to few chemicals and vinegar as the fabric softener. Wash on warm to help activate chemicals in the soap. After wash number two, throw the clothes into the dryer.

Sometimes, depending on the clothing itself and how potent it smells when it is removed from the packaging, I'll wash the clothing a few times before drying them.

Clothes that still smell fragrant or like chemicals can be hung on the clothes line outside to air out. A word of caution though...

**Clothesline It**

Hanging clothes out on the clothesline to help get rid of chemicals can be an effective way of getting rid of fragrance. In the sun's heat, some chemicals will "burn off" or off-gas more rapidly leaving the chemicals to dissipate into the outdoor air. If you're lucky enough to have clothes hanging on the line in the sun and the rain, the rain can help rinse some of the chemicals away.

We can't control Mother Nature, of course, so watch the weather and try to strategically plan ahead. Hang clothes out at night when it's supposed to rain and leave them out to dry in the sun, taking them off the line when you get home from work.

Caution though, you do not want to leave clothes on the clothesline too long. I've done this and am now the proud owner of multicolored clothing with a white line running through the middle of my shirts and dresses from sun fading and dark spots where the clothes were shaded from the sun. I call these clothes my weekend clothes, for days I don't go out in public.

Even hanging clothes on the line in winter is helpful. We Midwestern dwellers won't have rain in the winter, largely, unless it's freezing rain, but the sunshine in the winter is still effective.

## Strategic Buying

Over the years I've become more strategic about buying clothing. Instead of having *many* clothes that are made of cotton and natural materials, I have *fewer* clothes and those clothes are as chemical free as I can find. The pieces of clothing hanging in my closet did cost more per piece; however, buying less pieces of clothing offsets the cost.

The clothes I'm referring to have the GOTS Organic certification, or are from companies advertising their organic natural clothing has less dyes and finishes.

Debra Lynn Dadd is a seven-time author and internationally known consumer advocate on the topic of chemicals in consumer products. Over the years, Debra has created a list of companies selling "toxic free products" that is free to the public, called *Debra's List*. In my experience, clothing from

Debra's suggested companies have not had that new clothes smell or been an issue to wash and wear quicker than most standard clothing.

The number of companies listed crosses into the thousands. Clothing is one of the many types of products that Debra reviews, commenting on the material, dyes, and finishes used on clothing for each company listed. To search for clothing companies visit http://www.debralynndadd.com/debras-list/.

In addition to having fewer chemicals soaking into your skin all day and night, you'd be improving indoor air quality.

How does clothing fit into the topic of indoor air quality? By buying clothing with few to no chemicals, it helps to reduce the amount of chemicals coming into the home, your bedroom, and closet in the first place.

As a bonus, if you're buying fewer pieces of clothes, you're having less clothes collecting dust.

Why is that significant? Because dust is made up of itty bitty pieces of clothing fiber, microscopic plastic, dead bugs, and skin cells. It's dust from your electronics that becomes airborne when your computers and gaming stations fire up. It's dust from walking around the house. It's dirt, mold spores, and pollen brought in from the outdoors.

This dust has been found to contain chemicals that may be affecting our health.[128]

---

[128] Tasha Stolber, Jamee Hood, "How to Remove Toxic Dust, Your Home's Most Unwanted Guest," EWG News and Analysis, Environmental Working Group, November 9, 2017.

The more products in your home, including your clothing, the more dust is created and *captured*. That dust is re-circulating around your home, kicked up when you walk, and inhaled when you breathe indoor air. Given that the Environmental Protection Agency (EPA) estimates that people spend an average of 90% of their time indoors, you can get a sense of how important indoor air quality is.[129]

When you have fewer clothes in the closet, you have fewer clothes to wash up and fewer dust collectors. You can see the cycle this creates, how one affects the other. Like the yin and yang.

Every action has a reaction. If your action is to purchase clothing that has chemicals absorbing into your skin, off-gassing into the air, and circulating through house dust, the reaction may be developing one of the 140+ health conditions determined to be caused by chemicals in our everyday products.

The minimalist movement does not focus on living life with fewer chemicals, but it *does* focus on buying fewer products. The Minimalists[130] is a good resource for strategies on how to move from buying many things to buying fewer things.

To be a minimalist, you don't have to live in a 164-square-foot trailer. This group has a wide variety of members on

https://www.ewg.org/enviroblog/2017/11/how-remove-toxic-dust-your-home-s-most-unwanted-guest#.Wlzcj6inHIU

[129] "The Inside Story: A Guide to Indoor Air Quality," Indoor Air Quality, U.S. Environmental Protection Agency, Accessed February 27, 2017. https://www.epa.gov/indoor-air-quality-iaq/inside-story-guide-indoor-air-quality

[130] https://www.theminimalists.com/

their Facebook page, many of which are living in "typical" 1,800-square-foot homes but buying fewer products and just starting to become a minimalist by cleaning out one closet at a time. The online community is supportive of all people taking steps to buy fewer products.

## One.Step.At.A.Time. – Small Steps to Take to Make a Big Difference

Taking small steps can make a big difference towards living life with fewer chemicals. Replace clothing one piece at a time, as they wear out or you tire of wearing them. Use the steps below as a guide. Cross out the steps as you incorporate them into your life, and move on to whichever step you'd like to take next.

For example, if you're at the Just Starting level and your closet is 95% synthetic clothes (polyester, nylon, acrylic, etc.), then start by buying natural clothing (cotton, wool, linen, etc.). Cross #1 off the list. After buying a few pieces of natural clothing, pay attention to graphics and avoid vinyl or plastic graphics on t-shirts. Cross #2 off the list. Once you're comfortable with choosing natural clothing free of vinyl or plastic graphics, look for clothing that is one step better and does not have a special finish. Cross #3 off the list.
The next time you buy clothes, move on to Advanced #1 and buy 100% natural clothing.

Or, if it suits you better, start at Super Star to change your wardrobe from 95% synthetic clothes with finishes to 100% organic with no finishes. There's certainly nothing wrong that!

Just Starting:
1. Buy clothing made from a majority of cottons, linen, wools, and other natural materials vs. synthetics.
2. Avoid clothing with special finishes like "no iron," "wrinkle-free," and "stain resistant" clothing.
3. Avoid vinyl or plastic graphics on shirts. You should be able to feel the vinyl or plastic graphic on the shirt if it is made of either material (if shopping in stores).

Advanced:
1. Buy 100% natural material clothing such as cotton, linen, wool, and silk.
2. Mix clothing colors by buying natural clothing (without dyes) and light color clothing made with low-impact or plant-based dyes.
3. Avoid clothing with special finishes like "no iron," "wrinkle-free," and "stain resistant" clothing (still).
4. Buy water-resistant clothing that is cotton with a wax finish rather than vinyl or plastic.
5. Buy clothing with designs made from ink or embroidered graphics and text.

Super Star:
1. Look for the GOTS Organic labels.
2. Buy 100% organic clothing.
3. Buy clothing that is natural color (no dyes) or is dyed with natural dyes such as clay. If natural dyes are difficult to find, choose low-impact dyes.
4. Buy clothing free of finishes.
5. Skip the sequins and fake stones. Avoid added plastics on clothing.
6. Shop where the packaging is not plastic.

# Chapter 6
# Household Products

This category is a biggie. Household products can be anything from large appliances (refrigerator, stove, dishwasher, washer and dryer), small appliances (blenders, mixers), cookware, kitchen utensils, kitchen gadgets, garbage cans and bags, dish soaps and cleaning products, dishes and food storage, kid's toys, electronics and decorations—for starters.

The Campaign for Healthier Solutions and HealthyStuff.org teamed up to test 164 products purchased from four major discount retailers. Eighty one percent (81%) of the products (133 out of 164) contained at least one hazardous chemical above levels of concern, and 49% of products contained two or more.[131]

It's times like these where taking small steps to address one thing at a time is so important. This category alone can be overwhelming. But it doesn't have to be.

---

[131] HealthyStuff and Campaign for Healthier Solutions. "New Dollar Store Study Released." *EcologyCenter*, February 4, 2015.
https://www.ecocenter.org/article/hs-news-news/new-dollar-store-study-released

Let's break these down a bit and take a closer look at where chemicals can be found.

## Large Appliances

Take a look in your refrigerator. The interior is likely made of plastic.

When I was appliance shopping about four years ago, I remember opening one refrigerator door after another to find the perfect fridge. When I did, they reeked of plastic. Not only to me, who has a sensitive sense of smell, but to my significant other that can't smell jack crap. Even he commented, "Wow, that really smells like plastic." That's when I knew it was bad.

In addition to the plastics, fridge drawers come with a lubricant. Before the product is packaged for shipping, manufacturers put a lubricant on the drawer slides and the fruit and veggie drawers moisture level settings slide.

Stoves and ovens can be another source of chemicals. Whether it's a glass stove top or traditional burner, both models can contain chemicals. Ovens often come with a self cleaning setting. Don't use it. What happens is that the oven heats up the interior of the stove so hot that it actually off-gasses chemicals into the house.

I made that mistake with the first few stoves that I've had throughout the years. Even the instructions state to have good ventilation and suggest you leave the home. Well, there's a good reason for that. There are a lot of chemicals released when you do it.

To compound matters, the chemicals released into the air during stove cleaning are absorbed by other porous items in the home—drywall, cabinets, drapes, clothing, bedding, wood, plastics—and then those items re-off-gas those chemicals as well.[132]

To understand this concept better, let's look at cigarette smoke. If you're in a home where someone is smoking cigarettes and you come home smelling like smoke, those chemicals have been absorbed into your clothing and re-off-gas the smoke chemicals. With smoke it's easy to tell the chemicals are still present because they have a distinct odor to them. With other chemicals, such as stove cleaning chemicals, they are more difficult to smell making them harder to detect.

People generally don't feel good when they're exposed to oven self-cleaning. This is a good example of listening to your body—if you feel crumby when self-cleaning your oven, just don't do it. If you find an oven that does not have a self-cleaning setting, even better—buy it. Then there is no chance of anyone in your home accidentally turning it on.

Dishwashers have interiors made with plastic dish racks, utensil bins, and interior coatings that are plastic lined. That plastic heats up hot, hot, hot! If you've ever tried to remove your dishes immediately after the dry cycle, you know what I'm talking about. They're too hot to touch and remove from the dishwasher. That's how hot the plastic gets. And that heated plastic is off-gassing chemicals into the air in our homes.

---

[132] "Indoor Air Quality," Scientific Findings Resource Bank, Berkley Lab, Accessed January 12, 2018.
https://iaqscience.lbl.gov/voc-svocs

What happens is that the plastic heats up causing the plastic to off-gas (more than it does at normal temperature). Drying with the heat dry cycle causes the dishwasher to heat up again adding more off-gassing.

Similarly, washers and dryers are often times made with a significant amount of plastic. The exterior is usually metal, but the interior tub, drum and parts are often made of plastic. The plastic heats and gives off chemical gasses.

Small Appliances
Small appliances such as blenders, mixers, grinders, and juicers often come in plastic varieties.

Plastic containers on these small appliances can leach chemicals into food and off-gas chemicals into the air. When the internal parts such as the motor are working hard, working hard, working hard, it's heating up. As the motor heats up, the plastic heats up as well.

Now you have off-gassing of the plastic from just simply being plastic, and chemicals off-gassing from the heated plastic.

Cookware
Cookware comes in a variety of styles. Non-stick surfaces, commonly referred to as Tefalon surfaces, are a popular option for pots and pans.

Unfortunately, chemicals that are used to create the non-stick surfaces have been found in food and found to cause health conditions. Scientists have found these chemicals in nearly everyone's blood worldwide, in low amounts.[133]

What's commonly used with pots and pans? Kitchen utensils.

Kitchen Utensils
Who hasn't melted a plastic mixing spoon or two in their lifetime?

Even if it's not full-blown melted beyond recognition, plastic mixing spoons are known for softening or melting in food. Want proof? Look at the tip of a spatula. You'll often see that it's deformed, flattened, or squared at the end due to heat. Plastic mixing utensils soften, as any heated plastic would, as you're stirring your food.

As we know already, plastics are chock-full of chemicals by their very nature—it's a synthetic oil byproduct, which in plain English means man-made from chemicals and parts of crude oil.

Plus, chemicals like flame retardants have been found in cooking utensils.

Pile on the chemicals.

"We've analyzed 150 products for lead and metals, hazardous flame retardants and phthtalate plasticizers. What we found is that products with chemical hazards are still scattered

---

[133] "Teflon and Perfluorooctanoic Acid (PFOA), What are Teflon and PFOA? Where are they found?," What Causes Cancer, American Cancer Society, Last Revised January 5, 2016. https://www.cancer.org/cancer/cancer-causes/teflon-and-perfluorooctanoic-acid-pfoa.html

throughout the economy, in a wide variety of types of products. We found cooking utensils with brominate flame retardants, lead in jewelry and hazardous plasticizers in flooring and exercise equipment."[134]

Simply put, stay away from plastics.

Kitchen Gadgets
Along with kitchen utensils, gadgets are in a close category. Egg slicers, knife blocks, peelers are all examples of items that you can buy in plastic, metal, or wood varieties.

Garbage Cans & Bags
Kitchen and bathroom garbage cans are often plastic, or if they're not made of plastic, they have a plastic liner. More off-gassing.

Dish Soaps & Cleaning Products
When you think of cleaners, think of room by room, the cleaning supplies you use—dishwasher detergent, dish soap for pots and pans, toilet cleaner, spray cleaner that disinfects and deodorizes the counter, polish and conditioner for cleaning the stove, wood furniture polish, and kitchen sink scrub.

Take a moment to pause and consider this: what you're cleaning your kitchen counters and tables with, and your dishes and glasses with, is making contact with your food and beverages. Every single day.

---

[134] "Chemical hazards found in kitchen, exercise equipment, jewelry, consumer electronics, building and outdoor products. Some retailers responding, others remain silent," Fall 2013 Product Survey Results Released. HealthyStuff, November 15, 2013.
https://www.ecocenter.org/healthy-stuff/reports/fall-2013-product-survey-results-released

Residual, or leftover, chemicals sit on countertops. On the table. On the dishes. In the glasses.

When you eat off your plates or drink from your glasses, whatever you use as your dishwashing agent is mixed in with your food and beverages. When you cook your food, the food is sitting in pots and pans absorbing the residual cleaner.

Think about how you use your bathroom.

Do you set your toothbrush on the counter that you've cleaned with chemicals?

In our house, not only do our toothbrushes touch the counters but also sit in water puddles daily. Face washing, freshening up, or getting ready for bed ultimately results in water being splashed onto the counter around the sink.

As the water hits the counter, it mixes with chemical residue left behind by your cleaners. The "water" isn't just water at that point. It's water and whatever cleaner you use.

<u>Dishes & Food Storage</u>
Here's another easy shmeezie way to live life with fewer chemicals.

Ditch the plastic plates and cups. For the same reasons.

Storage containers, on the other hand, may take a little more time to part with. Plastic storage containers are handy, light, and convenient for storing and transporting food. They're relatively inexpensive, so if you lose or damage one, you simply throw it away (or recycle it) and get a different one without a lot of effort and cost.

Here's the trade off.

The plastic storage container is leaching into the food in a couple different ways: 1) Plastic is off-gassing into the air, so you have airborne chemicals, and 2) as you store the food in the container, the chemicals are being absorbed into the food itself.

Heated plastic off-gasses chemicals at a higher rate than room temperature plastic. To further compound matters, the heated food is melting the plastic too. You've seen plastic storage containers with puckered or warped bottoms? That's where the food got too hot and melted the plastic.

When heating food, never microwave food in a plastic container. Microwaving food heats food very rapidly to a high temperature.[135]

Moving to greener ground, my sister is notorious for reusing containers that food was packaged in—reusing and recycling plastic instead of buying new plastic storage containers. Cottage cheese containers have been reused for salad dressing many times over the years. It became a running joke in our family that she had the best plasticware around.

It stopped being funny when I learned this nugget: The plastic that those containers are often made of are not meant

---

[135] "EWG's Dirty Dozen: Cancer Prevention Edition," Rethink Cancer. Environmental Working Group, Accessed January 15, 2018. https://www.ewg.org/cancer/EWGs-dirty-dozen-cancer-prevention-edition.php#.WlzhGqinHIV

to be reused, so when you use them again and again, the plastic is actually breaking down and getting into your food supply at a greater rate.[136]

Green practices are not always healthy for people.

Kids' Toys

As I was learning about the chemicals in our everyday products, this was one of the shocking and unbelievable pieces of information I came across. Repeatedly.

Kids' toys contain many types of chemicals that are harmful to people's health. Particularly kids' health. Due to their size, behaviors, and time of growth and development, kids are more affected by chemicals in our everyday products than adults.[137] [138] This is downright disturbing.

Many kids' toys are made out of plastic or vinyl and can be harmful to human health (as described in the first few chapters). Toys can emit chemical fumes from paints, finishes, doll clothes, plastics, and foam. Common toys made of foam include foam blocks, pieces of foam to build a fort, dress-up gear, foam swords, and pool toys.

Yeah. It's even in places you'd never expect.

---

[136] Sophia Ruan Gushee, *A to Z of D-Toxing: The Ultimate Guide to Reducing Our Toxic Exposures.* (New York: The S File Publishing, LLC, 2015), 169.
[137] "Why Are Children Often Especially Susceptible to the Adverse Effects of Environmental Toxicants?," Principles of Pediatric Environmental Health. Agency for Toxic Substance & Disease Registry, February 15, 2016. https://www.atsdr.cdc.gov/csem/csem.asp?csem=27&po=3
[138] Minnesota Department of Health. "Chemicals of Special Concern to Children's Health." Children's Environmental Health. Accessed January 19, 2018.
http://www.health.state.mn.us/divs/eh/children/chemicals.html

On a not-so-surprising note, electronics used by kids and adults alike are another source for chemicals to reside.

Electronics
Computers, TVs, cellular phones, gaming stations, and other electronic devices contain chemicals in the computer parts and the inner workings of the electronic devices.

Starting with the insides of the electronics, you can find chemical flame retardants and other chemicals in computer systems.[139] Greenpeace found five categories of chemicals in computers made by popular companies.

When electronics run or are used, they heat up. Fans within the computer kick in to keep the device cool.

It's no secret that electronics contain plastic parts inside of them, and are housed in plastic casings. As the computer works throughout the day (and night), the plastic and chemicals in the computer are heated and off-gas more chemicals into the air, while generating computer dust. The fan blows dust containing flame retardants and other chemicals out of the computer system and into our indoor air.

Even though you don't see it with the naked eye shooting out of computers and TVs, it's there. One of the ways I know this is scientific evidence. Scientists have discovered flame

---

[139] GreenPeace, "Hazardous substances reduced but not eliminated from Laptops," Feature Story. October 23, 2007.
http://www.greenpeace.org/international/en/news/features/hazardous-substances-laptops/

retardants found in electronics and other products in the dust in the typical American home.[140]

Decorations

Picture frames, fridge magnets, artificial flowers, statues, and figurines make our homes "ours." They add personality to our homes and can make us feel worthy of inviting people over. Decorations are no exception to the group of household products that have been found to contain chemicals that may be harmful to health.

Standard picture frames are made from composite wood and pressed board material. Fridge magnets, artificial flowers, statues, and figurines are often made from vinyl and plastics.

While each item is small in size, the amount of items in a home can add up quickly. Typically, people don't have one statue or one picture frame. There are collages of framed pictures and full scenes of statues with artificial leaves winding between them. Wooden decorations made from plywood or pressed board and decorated with standard paints and finishes are found to off-gas VOCs.

One item could pack a punch, but many items likely have a larger impact.

---

[140] Tasha Stolber, Jamee Hood, "How to Remove Toxic Dust, Your Home's Most Unwanted Guest," EWG News and Analysis, Environmental Working Group, November 9, 2017.
https://www.ewg.org/enviroblog/2017/11/how-remove-toxic-dust-your-home-s-most-unwanted-guest#.Wlzcj6inHIU

## Solutions!

Unfortunately, there is not a third-party resource that measures the health of household products or says any particular five items, for example, have less chemicals (yet). That makes it a little trickier to choose products with less chemicals, but certainly not impossible.

Thanks to passionate people, there are online resources to help consumers find their way to retailers carrying products with fewer chemicals.

### Consumer Database

Debra Lynn Dadd is one of those people. For over thirty years, Debra has been researching and writing about how toxic chemicals affect our health and how to make safer choices as consumers. Her website includes the largest list of websites that sell toxic-free products, the largest Q&A, and recordings from the only talk radio show about toxics.[141]

Historically, I found her website to be interesting, informative, and helpful along my own journey to live life with fewer chemicals.

One way I have used Debra's website is to learn what others were buying for washing machines and dryers.

I had purchased a washer/dryer set that had such strong plastic off-gassing that I could not stand to keep the pair in my house. I visited Debra Lynn Dadd's website for guidance and read her Q&A and reader comments. Overwhelmingly, the Q&A revealed that washers and dryers have been a problem for many people, and the only washer and dryer that was consistently praised was the Speed Queen.

After buying one washer and dryer set that I couldn't use, I certainly didn't want a repeat, so I did a little further research to find that Speed Queen products are made of all metal exterior, parts, and interior stainless steel drum. It seemed to be my best option, so I invested in the set of Speed Queen appliances and have had success with them since.

It was helpful to know what worked well consistently for other people, and it helped me to narrow down my selection without wasting money investing in products that would off-gas chemicals into our home. It was a great way to avoid the most problem-ridden washers and dryers and invest in a set that consistently had the best track record for being a healthier product.

For products that don't have a third-party provider objectively assessing the healthiness of a product, we simply do the best we can do as consumers. Any step towards products with fewer chemicals is a great step.

**Avoid Plastic**
Simply put, buy non-plastic items whenever you can.

This solution can be applied to any product in this entire book, but as we take it one step at a time, here's how it relates to small appliances.

Blenders and mixers are just two of the many small appliances commonly found in kitchens that are often made with plastic. Alternatives are out there! You just have to know what to look for.

A bar blender is a type of all-stainless-steel blender and typically has metal gears versus plastic gears. They are more expensive than the plastic version, but they do not off-gas plastics into our foods and air and are typically more durable and longer lasting as well.

Mixers such as Kitchen Aids are made primarily from metal. Sometimes when they work hard, you'll smell the lubricant heat, so be aware of that. Compared to the plastic varieties, metal may still be a better option.

As we've discussed, they might be a little more expensive, but buying a few less items of healthier quality could lead to improved health and is one strategy that helps stay within the budget.

## Cook with Ceramics

You want to choose pots and pans that are healthier options. There are a few different materials out there.

Ceramic is the top choice of people looking to cook (or bake) with healthier cookware. Ceramic products that have been identified as healthier to cook with are 100% ceramic or have a blend of ceramic and glass. Products are made by smaller companies and major brand names alike and are available in retail stores and online. Of course, the ceramic must be lead-free to be healthy.

Cast iron has been debated in terms of being a healthy cooking product. Even though iron could leach into the food supply, some health experts argue that most Americans don't have enough iron in their food supply to begin with, so the iron, instead of being harmful, is somewhat helpful. Others state that they have concerns about iron leaching into food.

Stainless steel is another debated option for cookware. There are different compositions and grades of stainless steel. The composition describes the amount (percentage) and type of metal used to make the stainless steel product. Stainless steel is made with several types of metal, including chromium and nickel. The composition is listed on the cookware, typically on the underside of the pot or pan.[142]

Bottoms of pots, pans, and other stainless steel products are often stamped with a set of numbers like this: 18/8 or 18/10. The number indicates the amount of chromium and nickel in that particular type of stainless steel. For example, 18/8 means there is 18% chromium and 8% nickel in that stainless steel. The most common grade of stainless steel is 18/8, called Type 304.[143]

Where does 18/8 fall on the scale of good, better, best?

The grade of stainless steel indicates what the stainless steel can be used for. Even though stainless steel comes in over 150 different grades, over 70% is in the 300 series. Surgical stainless steel, Type 316, is often required for manufacturing

---

[142] "Stainless Steel Leaching Into Food and Beverages," Q & A. Debra Lynn Dadd, January 17, 2010.
http://www.debralynndadd.com/q-a/stainless-steel-leaching-into-food-and-beverages/

[143] "Stainless Steel Leaching Into Food and Beverages," Q & A. Debra Lynn Dadd, January 17, 2010.
http://www.debralynndadd.com/q-a/stainless-steel-leaching-into-food-and-beverages/

of food (and surgical matters) in order to minimize metallic contamination.[144]

Does this mean stainless steel can leach into food?

Yeah. It does.

When stainless steel is scratched, iron, nickel, and chromium can leach into food and drinks.[145]

I'd say the answer is simple—don't the scratch stainless steel. Perhaps easier said than done.

One way to at least reduce scratches to stainless steel, and ceramics for that matter, is to use wooden mixing utensils to cook food.

Cooking utensils come in stainless steel and wood varieties that do not melt when heated or leach chemicals into the food being cooked. And they are easy to find. Woot woot!

Egg slicers, knife blocks, and peelers are all examples of items that you can buy in either metal or wood varieties. Stainless steel spatulas, serving spoons, and ladles. Wooden spatulas, spoons, and salad servers. Glass or metal measuring cups.

---

[144] "Stainless Steel Leaching Into Food and Beverages," Q & A. Debra Lynn Dadd, January 17, 2010.
http://www.debralynndadd.com/q-a/stainless-steel-leaching-into-food-and-beverages/
[145] "Stainless Steel Leaching Into Food and Beverages," Q & A. Debra Lynn Dadd, January 17, 2010.
http://www.debralynndadd.com/q-a/stainless-steel-leaching-into-food-and-beverages/

You've got this.

Wood items that are unfinished or finished with linseed oil have the best chance of being nontoxic.

## Ceramic for Table Settings and Storage

Use ceramic or glass dishes and cups for meal time place settings. If breakability is a concern, buy stainless steel plates and cups as a durable alternative to plastic. Each of these options are affordable and readily available.

Storage can be a little trickier due to travel friendliness. Let's tackle the easiest step first.

Food that is not being transported (taken to work, parties, or picnics) can be easily stored in ceramic or glass containers with glass lids. Ceramic storage containers such as Casserole dishes are great for storing cooked veggies and other meals at home, but not great for travel, since they typically have looser fitting lids.

Another alternative option is to buy glass containers with fitted plastic lids that seal tight. These allow for transportation to places like parties, get-togethers, and picnics without too much hassle.

Stainless steel storage containers can be a good alternative to affordable light weight plastic used for day-to-day meals such as bringing lunches to work. These containers can be found online or in some health-conscious grocery stores.

When heating food, transfer food to a ceramic or glass dish/bowl/cup to microwave your food in. You could always heat it on the stovetop like they did back in the day.

## Clean Up the Garbage

Clean up the garbage can by trading plastic for metal or ceramic garbage cans. Believe it or not, metal and ceramic options are sold by retailers such as Kohl's, Bed Bath and Beyond, and Target and are easy to find.

Most metal garbage cans come with a plastic liner that can be removed. Just a heads up that the metal may not be fully liquid–proof, so liquids or juices will leak from the seams of the metal can. Speaking from experience, it's not a nice surprise to come home to.

The easiest fix is to separate food and wet garbage from dry garbage. Keep a one-gallon sealable plastic bag on the counter for food and wet garbage. Alternatively, re-use the plastic bags from frozen fruits and veggies as your daily food garbage bag. It's a low cost solution and avoids the need to buy and store multiple large plastic bags.

Dispose of the plastic food garbage bag every few days when it's full. As a bonus, this process helps keep the stench of rotting foods out of the house, eliminating the need for antibacterial and odor eliminating chemical sprays.

Alternatively, you could line the garbage can with a paper bag. Here, too, it's a little more work to pay attention to what's going into the garbage and when. Food and some wet garbage can be added, but preferably after absorbent or water proof garbage is disposed of, such as paper towels or plastic produce bags.

Paper bags are available at local grocery stores. You could bag groceries in paper and re-use the bag or purchase those paper bags for a small cost at some grocery stores if you prefer to have fresh, crisp, unused bags for garbage.

If you're not ready to ditch the plastic garbage liners, at least buy bags with the least amount of chemicals in them. Scented garbage bags can contain chemical fragrances that are releasing chemicals into your kitchen. You know by now, from previous chapters of this book, that fragrances are not good and to steer away from fragranced bags.

## Toys

When buying toys for your kids or others, consider what the toy is made from and the finishes—what's in it and on it.

Choose toys made from solid wood (preferably solid hardwood to avoid VOCs that may be off-gassing from soft woods), and ones that have adhesives, paints, stains, and finishes that are free of VOCs and other chemical toxins.

In 2015 PBS Kids® and Whole Foods Market (before it was purchased by Amazon) partnered to offer a line of toys called PlanToys® for children that were made out of wood and had nontoxic adhesives and paints that retail for under $30.

"These wooden toys are assembled using certified formaldehyde-free E-zero glue in place of traditional wood glue, and do not use chemical dyes containing lead or other heavy metals."[146]

---

[146] "PBS KIDS Partners with Whole Foods Market to Launch New Sustainable, Non-Toxic Toys This Holiday Season," Public Broadcasting Station. Press Releases, November 5, 2015.
http://www.pbs.org/about/blogs/news/pbs-kids-partners-with-whole-foods-market-to-launch-new-sustainable-non-toxic-toys-this-holiday-season/

How significant! It's just one example of companies working to make our everyday products healthier for consumers.

The trend towards less-chemical products is happening.

### Third-Party Testing & Database
When it comes to cleaners, the EWG website (or app if you have a smart phone) is the way to go. The database, EWG's Guide to Healthy Cleaning, shows health ratings of cleaning products that have been methodically reviewed and rated.

The number of products reviewed grows each year, now totaling over 2,500 products. Ratings are just like report card grades back in the day with "A" being great and "F" being not so great.

It's easy to use, and it's free.

The EWG website can also be used to look up health ratings of specific chemicals. This may come in handy if you're a DIYer.

### Become a DIYer
Do-It-Yourselfers have blogged recipes for nontoxic cleaners and personal care products such as deodorant, for a few years. Of course, just because it's DIY doesn't mean it's healthier for people. It does allow you to know all of the ingredients in a product though, which means you can determine for yourself if it truly is a healthier product.

Ingredients like white vinegar, baking soda, hydrogen peroxide, and lemon juice are well known for their safety and effectiveness in cleaning. Stick with DIY recipes where you know the ingredients are healthier. Or punch the ingredient name into the EWG website to read the health rating.

**Invest in a Good Air Purifier**

While you're working to reduce the number of chemicals in your home, invest in a good air purifier to help reduce the amount of harmful chemicals in the air. This is not a substitute for choosing products with fewer chemicals—buying natural products, all around, is the best way to a life with fewer chemicals. The air purifier is a tool that can complement your efforts and can be helpful no matter what stage of healthy you're striving for.

Two air purifiers that I've used are from Austin Air.

- Austin Air Healthmate Plus (+)
  The "plus" means that it filters chemicals such as SVOCs or VOCs that are emitted, or off-gassed, into the air by everyday products that contain chemicals. This full size machine filters up to 1,500 square feet of air. The amount of carbon in this machine can be problematic for some people with sensitivities. I know this based on my personal experience and a great, candid conversation with the amazingly helpful staff at Austin Air customer service.
- Austin Air Healthmate Plus (+) Jr.
  The junior plus version filters up to 700 square feet. Since it's smaller in size, the junior plus contains less carbon and may be a better option for people with sensitivities. It certainly was for me. It's also a great option for those of us with a limited budget or who want to test the purifier before investing in a larger version.

Start by filtering the air near bedrooms. We spend nearly a quarter of our time sleeping, more if you're a baby.

Adults need 7-9 hours of sleep per night, school-age children and teens need 9.5 hours per day, and babies need 16-18 hours per day.[147] During that time, our bodies are recovering and repairing themselves. By creating the healthiest bedroom environment and removing chemicals with an air purifier, it creates a better environment for your body to heal itself.

## Strategies
## Replace Items as Needed
One of the best strategies is to replace things as needed. This strategy was important to easily determine what to replace next, with healthier household items, while staying within my monthly budget.

When I say "as needed," I also mean "as wanted." Items that I was planning to buy anyway, even if they weren't worn out.

Perhaps you don't need to replace a kitchen gadget, but it would be oh-so-fun to have a new kitchen gadget. Buy the gadget with fewer chemicals in it. Maybe you buy an all-metal set of measuring cups instead of the plastic ones.

## See Value in Aged Items
I wouldn't go out and buy all new appliances tomorrow by any means.

---

[147] "Brain Basics; Understanding Sleep," National Institute of Neurological Disorders and Stroke. https://www.ninds.nih.gov/Disorders/Patient-Caregiver-Education/Understanding-Sleep

Generally, if items don't need to be replaced, then don't replace them. As time goes on, chemicals that are off-gassing from furniture, appliances, plastics, and other household items become less.

If a product is not damaged or broken, consider keeping the product to avoid buying products that can off-gas chemicals into your home. By all means, please do replace items that are broken or damaged or on their last leg. Replace them with products that contain fewer chemicals.

## Small & Large Dollars

Mix low cost purchases with large cost purchases. This more consistent approach to buying and replacing items keeps the budget balanced easier and helps to avoid a big impact on your budget down the road. Perhaps the month that you replace the washer and dryer, you buy a stainless steel fry pan.

Watch store closeout sales for household items that are made with fewer chemicals. Pick up one or two wooden mixing spoons if they're on sale. Small changes have a big impact over time. Every little bit matters.

## Old School

The trend towards living life with fewer chemicals is really about going back to basics, kickin' it old school. I don't mean old school in that you should hang a disco ball in your living room, but old school like solid wood furniture and ceramic dinnerware.

Cleaners like vinegar, baking soda, and lemon juice have been used for YEARS without harming people's health. To have products around that long and not have it be harmful to human health, and without controversy, says a lot! They have stood the test of time. And that's huge.

## Electronics

In terms of chemicals, Apple products contained the least amount of chemicals according to Greenpeace's recently released report, *Guide to Greener Electronics 2017*.[148] The report ranked 17 major electronics companies on three categories: chemicals in electronics, resources, and energy.

When considering all three categories, Fairphone earned the highest score with Apple products being a close second. In terms of chemicals, Apple earned the highest score followed by Fairphone.

Use the information to your advantage! It's easy to read, even for us average Joes that have not memorized chemical names.

Access the report at http://www.greenpeace.org/usa/reports/greener-electronics-2017/.

## Decorating

There's an alternative way to spice up your home while avoiding chemicals in everyday products. Decorate using colored paint. Using paints with fewer chemicals, of course.

A friend and former colleague of mine, Cindi, had (and still has) an interior design business. One day at work she mentioned that her next project was to paint her dining room two different shades of green, purple, and gold. I am a

---

[148] http://www.greenpeace.org/usa/

person that does not hide my true feelings well, and for the life of me, I could not understand how that was going to look good. I can only imagine what my expression looked like.

After the room was complete, Cindi had a few people over to see her finished product. I was amazed, absolutely amazed, at how colorful, decorative, and tactful the room looked. And with very few pieces of decoration. The only wall accessories in the entire room were a mirror and a metal decoration beside it.

It was amazing how using just the right colors strategically placed was enough to have the entire room look decorated. It was really something to see.

For must-have decorations, follow the principals of buying ceramic, metal, or wood with no- or low-VOC finishes and fewer chemicals overall.

Ceramic figurines come in different shapes, styles, and finishes and are pretty easy to find. Choose unfinished solid hardwood frames and paint or finish them yourself using no- or low-VOC paints and finishes, or metal or ceramic frames. Mirrors come unframed or can be framed in metal frames.

Most mainstream retail companies carry these healthier decoration options. You just have to know what to look for.

So how do you do this? How do you start changing your household products over to healthier items? This is a big category to tackle. Take it one step at a time.

## One.Step.At.A.Time.

Just Starting:

1. Each month, remove one household item that is worn out or that is plastic. Replace the item with glass, ceramic, or wood finished with nontoxic finishes. OR, don't replace it at all. If it's not an item being used, then there is no need to replace it!
2. Choose an easy to find item like dishware or drinking glasses and switch to ceramic or glass.
3. Store leftover food in glass or ceramic containers.
4. Buy healthier toys for kids.

Advanced:

1. Replace 50% of plastic items with glass, ceramic, or wood finished with nontoxic finishes.
2. Scale back the number of items in your home to reduce the amount of items off-gassing in your home, reduce the amount of dust generated (which contains chemicals found in everyday products), and reduce the amount of surfaces for dust to settle on.
3. Use 50% of cleaning supplies that are made from natural ingredients or rated as healthier.

Super Star:

1. 95% of household items made of plastic are removed from your home or replaced.
2. 95% of opportunities for buying nontoxic household items were used to indeed buy healthier items.
3. 100% of cleaning supplies have been changed to vinegar, baking soda, nontoxic soaps, hydrogen peroxide, or one that is rated as a "A" or "B" in EWG's Guide to Healthy Cleaning database.

# Chapter 7
# Personal Care Products

When I first read, "Would you put Teflon on your face?" I wondered to myself, whaaaat is thiiiissss!?

The report funded by the Breast Cancer Fund goes on to say, "Did you know some anti-aging creams and face powders use the same chemical that create a nonstick surface on cookware to create a smooth finish to makeups and lotions?"

Well, now I do!

How did I not know this before?

As it turns out, companies don't have to list all of the ingredients on product labels. If they say it's a "trade secret," then they don't have to disclose the ingredients to the public.[149]

---

[149] "Trade Secret Policy," United States Patent and Trademark Office, May 11, 2016.
https://www.uspto.gov/patents-getting-started/international-protection/trade-secret-policy

A report from the EWG found 38 chemicals not listed on the labels of 17 name-brand products. Each product had an average of 14 unlisted chemicals in them.[150]

The Campaign for Safer Cosmetics website[151] shows 39 chemicals found in cosmetics that have been identified by scientists as having adverse health effects.[152]

In the U.S., our personal care products can have more harmful chemicals than the EU version of the exact.same.product.[153] Yeah. Crazy.

## **Where are Chemicals Found**

The European government has banned some chemicals that scientists have linked to health risks. We have a lipstick with harmful chemicals that is sold in the United States, and the same lipstick without harmful chemicals that is sold in Europe.

That's really disappointing, first of all, and secondly, it's an example of how in the U.S. we have a long way to go. So, how do you choose personal care products that have less chemicals?

---

[150] Environmental Working Group and the Campaign for Safe Cosmetics, "Hidden Chemicals in Perfume and Cologne," Not So Sexy. May 12, 2010.
[151] http://www.safecosmetics.org/
[152] "Anti-Aging Secrets Exposed, Chemical Linked to Breast Cancer in Skin Care," Breast Cancer Fund, Campaign for Safe Cosmetics, October 2015. http://www.safecosmetics.org/wp-content/uploads/2015/10/Anti-aging-secrets-exposed-report.pdf
[153] Young, Saundra, "Endangering the Next Generation of Brains," Our Toxic Times. Chemical Injury Information Network, March 2014, Volume 25, Number 3: 2-3.

In order to determine where we as consumers should start, it's important to understand where these chemicals can be found.

## Fragranced Products

Fragrance can be made from *any number* of the 3,100 chemicals that are standardly used in the fragrance industry. Manufacturers can list fragrance ingredients as simply "fragrance" without naming which chemicals have been used to make the fragrance or scent.[154]

Where can fragrances be found?

Perfume, cologne, and body sprays are the first that come to mind—the entire product is one big fragrance. However, fragrances are found in many of the products that we use daily. Body and face soap. Shampoo and conditioner. Bath salts. Body and hand lotion. Laundry detergent and fabric softener.

Stores and restaurants have spray machines in the public bathrooms and on the retail floor that spray fragrance into the air at certain times.

Beyond fragrance, personal care products can contain many other chemicals that may be harmful to health.

---

[154] "Hidden Chemicals in Perfume and Cologne," Not So Sexy. Environmental Working Group and the Campaign for Safe Cosmetics, May 12, 2010. https://www.ewg.org/research/not-so-sexy#.Wfn3x2hSzlU

## Lotions, Cosmetics, Toothpaste, Hair Styling

Of the over 100,000 chemicals in our everyday products, it's estimated that 1:7 is used in personal care products.[155] A quick calculation shows that's 14,285 chemicals that are estimated to be used in personal care products.

The types of products where these chemicals can be found are:

- Lotions
- Cosmetics such as mascara, blush, foundation, eye shadow, lipstick, chap stick, foundation, and more
- Toothpaste
- Hair styling products such as hair sprays, gels, mousse, dyes, perms, straighteners. Often times if you go into a salon, the smell of hair styling chemicals is overpowering. It can make your eyes burn. Those are the types of chemicals we're talking about.
- Soaps such as shampoo, conditioner, body soap, and hand soap
- Deodorant

These products sit on your skin and scalp soaking into the body and being breathed in all day long. The same products that are meant to keep us clean and healthy may be causing health issues.

## Feminine Care Products

In addition to the standard personal care products that men and women use, women spend about six days of the month

---

[155] Sophia Ruan Gushee, *A to Z of D-Toxing: The Ultimate Guide to Reducing Our Toxic Exposures.* (New York: The S File Publishing, LLC, 2015), 274.

using feminine care products—over 40 years.[156] That's 2,880 days over the span of 40 years.

Standard feminine care products are made from synthetic material (polyester) which is an oil byproduct found in both the covering and filling, contain chemical and fragrances, and have plastic backings and packaging.

As we know, the plastic off-gasses and is absorbed by the product inside, being a porous product. Of course, maxi pads are meant to absorb things! Including the chemicals they are exposed to.

Women's Voices for the Earth[157] made a video called "Detox the Box" that was shown on Saturday Night Live to get the point across that there are chemicals in feminine care products AND to put the pressure on mainstream companies to get chemicals out of feminine care products—hence, "detox the box."

## Hair Styling Tools

Hair styling tools such as hair brushes, blow dryers, and hair straighteners are made from plastic, a material that off-gasses chemicals into the air at normal temperatures. Of course, if they were made of all metal we'd burn ourselves using them.

---

[156] "What's happening during the typical 28-day menstrual cycle?," Office on Women's Health, U.S. Department of Health and Human Services. Page last updated October 16, 2017.
https://www.womenshealth.gov/menstrual-cycle/your-menstrual-cycle#3
[157] https://www.womensvoices.org/

With plastic, we don't burn ourselves, but we do promote the release of toxic chemicals by heating the plastic. When plastic is heated, it off-gasses at an increased amount.

If you're blow drying your hair, you often use a brush to either help style the hair in a certain way or to break up the hair a bit so that it can be dried faster.

Curling irons and flat irons have a metal or ceramic plate that can have a Teflon finish or coating on the iron surface. When that coating is heated, just like plastic, it can off-gas chemicals in higher amounts.

Hair clips and ponytail holders are often made of plastic and polyester, nylon, spandex, or rubber that my contain chemicals.

## Toothbrush
Standard toothbrushes are made from plastic with nylon bristles. Both are synthetic materials made from oil byproducts and may be causing health conditions.

## Solutions!
### Steer Away from Plastics
Avoid plastics whenever you can. Hair brushes and tooth brushes made with wooden handles with natural bristles are one option. Be aware that hair brushes that are cushioned may contain rubber. Sometimes the natural products will give off a natural odor which some people don't like.

In this case, choose an all-hard-plastic hair brush (with no cushy plastic or foam on the handle). Plastic in general is an oil byproduct and does off-gas chemicals, but if buying plastic is a must, stick to hard plastic which typically contains less chemicals than soft plastic.

## Trade Perfume for (specific) Essential Oils

Perfume is a big one. If you wear it, especially every day, this may be a high-priority on your list of things to change.

Now, there are people that feel like perfume is part of who they are, part of their being. I've had a number of people in my life that when I asked them to not wear perfume, fragrance, or body spray, they told me that they just couldn't do that. It's part of their routine in the morning and part of what makes them who they are. And that's okay.

Sometimes people wear fragrances to mask medical conditions, such as body odor that they haven't been able to get under control. Everybody is unique. Everybody is individual. And everybody has to do what's right for them.

If fragrances are a must-have, use essential oils that are made from natural ingredients. It is a common misperception that all essential oils are safe for people. Some essential oils are made from chemical mixtures, just like standard perfumes, colognes, and body sprays.

Purchase essential oil brands that have the USDA Organic label on them or have been tested by a third-party for their effect on health.

## No Added Fragrances

Nearly every personal care product that has fragrances added comes in a non-fragrance variety. These products are often labeled as fragrance-free, unscented, or free and clear.

Ideally, by avoiding fragranced products (and the chemicals used to make fragrances), these products would have fewer chemicals in them. However, just because it says fragrance free doesn't mean it's healthy.

"Fragrance free," "unscented," or "free and clear" products can mean one of two things: no fragrance was added, or a neutral fragrance was added. Neutral fragrances are intended to hide the smell of other ingredients.[158]

It's sort of maddening that companies are allowed to do this. It makes it frustrating for consumers such as you and I that are working to live life with fewer chemicals. But it is the reality of our world today.

And so, while it may not be perfect, choosing personal care products that are unscented is still a big step in the direction of living life with fewer chemicals.

## USDA Organic Seal

While the U.S. Food and Drug Administration is in charge of regulating cosmetics,[159] the U.S. Department of Agriculture (USDA) is responsible for regulating the term "organic," including organic cosmetics and other personal care products.[160] Certification of organic personal care products

---

[158] Sophia Ruan Gushee, *A to Z of D-Toxing: The Ultimate Guide to Reducing Our Toxic Exposures.* (New York: The S File Publishing, LLC, 2015), 189.

[159] U.S. Food & Drug Administration. "Small Businesses & Homemade Cosmetics; Fact Sheet." Cosmetics. Accessed January 19, 2018. https://www.fda.gov/cosmetics/resourcesforyou/industry/ucm388736.htm#7

[160] United States Department of Agriculture, Agricultural Marketing Service. National Organic Program. "Cosmetics, Body Care Products, and Personal Care Products." April 2008. https://www.ams.usda.gov/sites/default/files/media/OrganicCosmeticsFactShe et.pdf

follows the same rules as certifications for food and beverages.

The USDA has four organic labeling categories.
- 100% Organic – labeled as "100 percent organic"
- 95%-100% Organic – labeled as "organic"
- 70% or more Organic – labeled as "made with organic ingredient"
- Less than 70% organic – no label indicating organic, but organic ingredients can be listed as such

Look for the USDA Organic symbol on personal care products to find products made with 95%-100% organic ingredients.

## Hair Clips & Ponytail Holders
Hair-holding devices can be found in metal, cotton, or organic cotton varieties. You could make your own headbands by buying organic cotton fabric and sewing a few seems, relatively easy. If you're like me and think "no way Josè," you can look for these alternatives...

Metal hair clips. Metal hair accessories are often made of metal that has nickel in it, which some people are sensitive to. Gold hair clips made from 14-karat gold can be found in some mainstream department or jewelry stores and may be a good alternative for those sensitive to nickel.

Ponytail holders. Cotton or organic cotton ponytail holders can often be found in health-conscious stores and even some mainstream online stores.

Bandanas. Not only for the 80s and 90s trend setters, bandanas made of organic cotton can be used to protect from the sun, hold hair back, and catch sweat while working hard. Follow the guidelines for buying clothing (consider material, dyes, finishes) found in Chapter 5 when choosing bandanas.

## Don't Do It

Simply put, if it's unhealthy for you, then don't do it. Don't buy it or use it. View personal care products as a piece of your health. When healthier alternative products aren't available, find creative solutions that allow you to still live life with fewer chemicals by simply avoiding the harmful product.

For example, if there is no healthier alternative on the market for curling irons and hair straighteners that can off-gas chemicals and may affect health, find a hairstyle that doesn't require those tools to be used.

Or if you currently apply 10 standard personal care products a day, consider reducing that number to five personal care products per day. Eliminate those products that are difficult to find with healthier ingredients and continue with the products that have fewer chemicals.

## Strategies
### Notice Patterns

Our bodies give us hints all of the time, as we discussed in Chapter 3. We just have to pay attention to the patterns to figure out what our bodies are telling us. This was the case when I first realized how feminine care products were affecting my own health.

Being the diligent buyer of products with less chemicals in them, I purchased maxi pads from a company that was well known in the "natural product" community. The packaging stated "made with organic cotton."

Each month when I used the maxi pads, I'd break out in quarter-sized welts that hurt to touch. Now, I'm no doctor by any stretch of the imagination, but I knew that breaking out in painful welts wasn't a good thing.

When I really started paying attention to where the welts were, I noticed they made a pattern around the edge of where the maxi pad was.

The pattern repeated itself month after month. Clearly an indication that something wasn't quite right.

At my annual checkup I mentioned this to my doctor as one of my concerns. I said to him, "I'm really stumped though. This product says organic cotton, so I don't know what's going on here. I don't know if it's the adhesive or packaging it's in or what."

He replied, and this is one of the things I love about my doctor, "I wonder what's in that product."

Let that sink in for a moment.

My doctor was reinforcing the idea that our bodies are wise and can tell us when something isn't quite right.

Secondly, his comment caused me to go home and re-read the package. Maybe I had missed something. I didn't know what was going on, but I knew for sure that this monthly experience was not any fun.

As it turned out, the package did mention organic cotton, but said that it had organic cotton *covering*. The ingredients list showed polyester as the filling. Mystery solved.

Patterns can appear when using any number of products. Some patterns are tougher to pinpoint than others, especially when several products are causing the problem.

Start by paying attention to how you feel when you use a certain personal care product. Then stop using it for a short time. And then use it again.

Did you notice a difference in how you feel? If you can recreate the problem, that's a good indicator of the products that may be causing the issue.

The process of noticing patterns is ongoing. When one source is fixed, several more patterns may appear causing you to notice how chemicals in our everyday products may be affecting your health.

The process is like peeling an onion. One layer or toxic product is removed, but that's just the first of many layers to be addressed. As you continue to peel back the layers, you'll realize just how much better you feel. And what the true causes were for feeling yucky.

## Use Third-Party Verified Sites

I'm not a big fan of looking for and understanding specific chemical names, but I do believe it's important to understand the overall idea that there are chemicals in our everyday products. AND I am more focused on finding trusted companies and using products verified or certified by third-party nonprofit resources.

It's lucky for consumers like you and I that there are places out there like the EWG that have a database of over 70k personal care products that they have analyzed and assigned a health rating to. Consumers can either search by brand or product or sort by rating and look for the products with a 1 through 10 rating.

The database includes products such as soaps, shampoos, cosmetics, sunscreens, perfumes, toothpastes, hair styling products, feminine care products, and deodorants—most of the items mentioned in this chapter.

There's also an app that allows you to stand in the store and scan the barcode on a product, and the EWG app brings up the health rating of the product. This database is available to the public for free. For FREE. That's incredible.

Recently, EWG started certifying products that meet EWG's strictest criteria. The products are called EWG Verified products and have the EWG logo on them.

Get the app. Use the data. Look for EWG Verified products. It's just that valuable.

Made Safe[161], is another nonprofit organization that provides third-party verification of products that have fewer chemicals. Instead of rating products, Made Safe certifies products that they determine as being safe for people.

Their website has a list of products that meet the Made Safe certification criteria. Made Safe's list of certified products is free to the public, too!

Get searching!

## Places to Shop

Another resource that is helpful, but is a for-profit company (not a 501c3 not-for-profit such as the EWG) is Debra Lynn Dadd.[162] For full disclosure, Debra does accept payment from companies that ask her to review products, as stated on her website. I am not clear on the exact method she uses; however, I have personally found her website and resources helpful in my own journey of living life with fewer chemicals.

Debra's website is the most comprehensive resource I've found that lists companies carrying products with fewer chemicals in them. She has links to companies selling personal care products, clothing, furniture, water filters, and more.

## Ask Stores for Products

If you find a healthier product, but your local stores don't carry the item, ask your local store to carry it.

Over the years I've asked several stores in our area to carry a specific product on their shelf. Sometimes it was well

---

[161] https://madesafe.org/
[162] http://www.debralynndadd.com

received and sometimes it was not. You never know until you ask!

In instances where the store won't carry the product permanently, or you don't want to buy it regularly, ask if they'll special order the product for you. Many times stores will have access to a lot more products than are on their shelves.

Their warehouse, suppliers, and distribution center may have products available that are not stocked in your specific store. You may have to buy the item in larger quantities, so be sure to ask before ordering the item.

## Online Ordering

Online stores make healthier products more easily available. You can find a healthier product in the EWG database, search for it on any online store, and buy it right then and there.

Online shopping allows you to easily compare prices as well, which can be helpful for those of us buying healthier products on a budget.

## Buy Fewer Products

Generally speaking, less products with fewer chemicals can make a really big impact. Instead of having three different shades of mascara (black, dark brown, and brown), you just have one shade of mascara and that particular shade can be the healthiest option that is available to you.

This idea can be applied across all types of personal care products, too. For example, some people will buy scented lotion and perfume. That's a whole lotta scent goin' on if you wear them together. Consider buying either the lotion or the perfume.

Or buying one product with fragrance and one without. Any way to reduce the number of products, and the number of products with chemicals, the better.

This next one seems counter to what I just said, but it's completely aligned.

**Buy in Larger Quantities**
Of the healthier products that you DO choose to buy, purchase them in larger quantities to take advantage of free shipping and quantity discounts. I'm not saying be wasteful or buy items you don't need. Take advantage of the offer by placing larger orders less frequently. Online stores often times have free shipping offers for purchases over a certain dollar amount.

Place an order for personal care products once a month or once every other month, but order quantities that will last you until the next order. For example, I will order three shampoos, three conditioners, two body soaps, and two toothpastes at one time in order to meet minimum shipping costs. I place the order when I'm running low to allow enough time (usually a few days) for the order to arrive.

While I order higher quantities, I still limit the quantity to the amount I feel comfortable storing in our house and feel confident that we will consume. There is no sense in buying in such large quantities that the products collect a year's worth of dust and tie up precious budget dollars if you don't need the product.

Find the balance between ordering in quantities large enough to have a financial incentive (free shipping or quantity discount) but not so large that it takes over your cabinet space or ties up income needed to pay other bills. Most personal care products don't go bad in 30 or 60 or 90 days which allows plenty of time to use the products.

Places like N.E.E.D.S. (Nutritional Ecological Environmental Delivery System)[163] generally sell healthier products, and sometimes offer quantity discounts. If you decide to buy enough to qualify for a quantity discount, ask friends or family if they're interested in going halvsies with you. Suddenly your 12 shampoos at 10% off may become more manageable both budget-wise and storage-wise.

## Replace One at a Time

Work these products into your life one step at a time. As your standard old products run out, replace them with products that have fewer chemicals. This is contrary to the advice of some, but it was a method that has been proven to work well and worked for me personally.

I didn't clear out my shelves. I didn't throw away all of our soaps and lotions and toothpaste and hair styling products and feminine care products. I didn't wipe us out.

I just started replacing with healthier options as my old products started running out on their own. This method helps to minimize being overwhelmed while automatically helping to prioritize the items you use most.

---

[163] https://www.needs.com

Chances are you will run out of items like hand soap, face soap, body soap, shampoo, and conditioner first since they are items used every day by most people. When our hand soap ran out, I replaced it with a hand/face/body soap that had a health rating of "1" from the EWG.

Plus buying one type of soap versus three was far more efficient and economical.

**Tackle Products You Use Most**

In prioritizing, you want to tackle the products that you use most and those that are sitting on your skin and soaking in every day all day. Soaps, deodorants, cosmetics, lotions.

Replace the products you use every single day versus products you use part of the year or occasionally, first. Then work your way to the next-most-used item.

**Low Cost Changes**

Low cost changes like new toothpaste and a new toothbrush is next on the priority list of things to alter. It's pretty easy to change these items and has a relatively low budget impact.

Think of how many times you buy a tube of toothpaste or toothbrush—the latter being far less often. It's not super often and the amount that you use is relatively small compared to soaps, lotions, and cosmetics.

**Create Cues to be Successful**

Create cues or reminders for yourself in order to remember to choose products with fewer chemicals.

One of the ways to do this is by placing online orders for healthier personal care products at the same time of the month. On the first Sunday of the month, plan time to meet with your family and identify what items need to be ordered, look up suggestions for healthier products, and add them to the list.

If you laughed at the idea of your family sitting down and ordering items together once per month because it's typically running in different directions, you're not alone. Here are two great time-saving methods that we've used in our house.

Print a list of items you typically order and hang it on the fridge. Include a line titled "Less Chemicals: _____." This is where you'll write which product you're going to buy that has fewer chemicals.

Before sitting down to order, check your cabinets to see which items and quantities you need to order. Leave room for "other" items that the family can add to as they think of them. That way everyone has an opportunity to write their requests, and the list is ready when you are ready to order, at any given moment.

Encourage family members to find products with less chemicals in them. Make it a family affair.

Alternatively, each Sunday start a shopping list of items needed that week. Split the list into two columns: online order and grocery store. Include a line titled "Less Chemicals: _____" in each column.

During the week find one personal care product that has less chemicals and add it to the list. Leave the list on the table until Friday (or Saturday or whatever day) when you go shopping. The list will be ready for you at any given moment and can be used for online ordering or grocery shopping.

Look for your less-chemical item at your local store and if you don't find it there, look it up online when you get home.

**Encourage Corporations to Remove Chemicals**
Some big companies are taking harmful chemicals out of their personal care products. We have a looooong way to go, but there is movement, which is SO exciting. Here are a few manufacturers and retailers that are removing chemicals from their products:

> "Johnson & Johnson recently made good on its commitment to phase out the use of a range of harmful chemicals in its baby products and is expected to reformulate its adult products by the end of 2015."[164]

> "In 2008, when Walmart—the world's largest retailer—agreed to stop selling baby bottles, sippy cups and sports water bottles made with BPA, it forced manufacturers to reformulate in order to keep selling to this retail giant"[165]

> "More and more retailers are adopting storewide policies governing the safety of their beauty products,

---

[164] "Anti-Aging Secrets Exposed, Chemical Linked to Breast Cancer in Skin Care," Breast Cancer Fund, Campaign for Safe Cosmetics, October 2015. http://www.safecosmetics.org/wp-content/uploads/2015/10/Anti-aging-secrets-exposed-report.pdf
[165] "Anti-Aging Secrets Exposed, Chemical Linked to Breast Cancer in Skin Care," Breast Cancer Fund, Campaign for Safe Cosmetics, October 2015. http://www.safecosmetics.org/wp-content/uploads/2015/10/Anti-aging-secrets-exposed-report.pdf

with Whole Foods leading the way by implementing a basic chemical safety screening for all its personal care products and adopting a restricted-substances list made up of more than 400 chemicals prohibited from products bearing its premium standards label."[166]

"In 2008 CVS stepped up to the plate by adopting a storewide policy prohibiting the use of certain toxic chemicals in their store-brand baby products. Walgreens and Target followed suit in 2013 by announcing they would develop and adopt comprehensive cosmetic safety policies to govern the safety of the private-label and national brands they carry."[167]

Organizations that partner with the Campaign for Safer Cosmetics[168] are working to remove harmful chemicals linked to health issues and found in personal care products. Made Safe, a partner of the Campaign for Safer Cosmetics, has a list of brands that are Made Safe certified on their website.

Two more tools that we can all use at no cost.

---

[166] "Anti-Aging Secrets Exposed, Chemical Linked to Breast Cancer in Skin Care," Breast Cancer Fund, Campaign for Safe Cosmetics, October 2015. http://www.safecosmetics.org/wp-content/uploads/2015/10/Anti-aging-secrets-exposed-report.pdf

[167] "Anti-Aging Secrets Exposed, Chemical Linked to Breast Cancer in Skin Care," Breast Cancer Fund, Campaign for Safe Cosmetics, October 2015. http://www.safecosmetics.org/wp-content/uploads/2015/10/Anti-aging-secrets-exposed-report.pdf

[168] http://www.safecosmetics.org

## One.Step.At.A.Time.

Just Starting:

1. Reduce the number of fragranced products that you use. Choose "free and clear" type products.
2. Reduce the amount of times you wear perfume, body spray, or cologne to only special occasions.
3. Create cues such as a shopping list that has a line for "less chemical item," reminding you to look for that item in a version that has fewer chemicals.

Advanced:

1. 50% of personal care products are made with natural and organic products or have a health rating of "A," "B," or "C" from EWG.
2. Find and use two new products per week that have fewer chemicals in them.
3. 50% of personal care products are absent of fragrance.

Super Star:

1. 95% of personal care products such as lotions, cosmetics, toothpaste, hair styling, deodorant, and feminine care products are made with natural organic products or have a health rating of "A" or "B" on EWG's Skin Deep Guide to Cosmetics or are an EWG Verified product.
2. All personal care products used are fragrance free.
3. Get involved in encouraging corporations to create more products with fewer chemicals. Join efforts of Campaign for Safe Cosmetics,[169] Women's Voices For the Earth,[170] or similar organizations that influence companies that make personal care products to make them with fewer chemicals.

---

[169] http://www.safecosmetics.org/
[170] https://www.womensvoices.org/

# **Chapter 8**
# **Lifestyle Change**

Living life with fewer chemicals is a lifestyle change. And like any lifestyle change, you will encounter naysayers and challenges but also reap the rewards of becoming the YOU that you want to be.

In the words of an anonymous author who's wisdom hangs on our refrigerator,

> "Life isn't about finding yourself.
>
> Life is about creating yourself."

Creating a life with fewer chemicals is becoming easier, with more people every day becoming aware and wanting to live healthier happier lives. But there are still challenges.

**Naysayers**
Naysayers are people that don't believe, don't understand, or simply don't care about chemicals in everyday products and their links to health effects. I've heard comments like, "I'm too old to be worried about it," "This is how life is for everyone," and "It's old age (at age 30)."

When I made a lifestyle change to living life with fewer chemicals, I wanted to think that every one of my family, friends, and colleagues would understand, be supportive, and be interested in this change I was making. Especially since it had such a large impact on my (and my son's) health.

Truth be told, that wasn't the case.

I've heard similar experiences time and time again when people make lifestyle changes of any kind, even life changes that are well understood and easily achievable.

My friend Mike was a diabetic (Type 2 Diabetes), had a heart condition, and had been hospitalized several times with pneumonia. His doctor told him that he needed to turn his life around—to start eating healthier and exercising, even if it was just getting out for a walk. He needed to do something to get moving and start living a healthier life.

During one of our conversations, Mike, visibly anguished, told me he was torn about making this life change. Thinking that choosing between life and death was a no brainer, I asked, "Why wouldn't you just take small steps to start eat healthier and start exercising?"

His answer: "I'll lose my friends and family, and they are my life."

Mike was a social butterfly, pouring his heart into everything he did. He was a person that saw his job as building relationships and helping people achieve their greatest potential. This also meant that his social schedule required that he went out to eat five to six times per week.

I suggested that he eat salad with chicken and one beer instead of a double burger, fries, and many beers. He tried it. But it didn't last long. Mike's friends started making fun of him, razzing, "What's a big guy like you eating a salad for," "That can't possibly fill you up," and "What do you mean you're only having one drink tonight?"

On top of that, he felt that his wife was not supportive of his changes. She would buy junk food and bring it into the house, despite his requests not to. He struggled to resist the temptation every single moment he was at home.

Fast forward six months.

Mike had a heart attack.

And survived.

Hospitalized from heart surgery and recovering from pneumonia, his doctors said, "If you don't take this very seriously, you are going to die. You have to change your eating. You have to change your lifestyle. Or you will die." Finally, he started to take his health more seriously, taking walks and improving his eating.

Then he lost his job.

And when he lost his job, he decided that the only important thing in life was living a lifestyle being surrounded by people that he loved and cared about—his family, friends, unhealthy food, and unhealthy habits. He went back to eating out five to six times a week eating burgers and beers and oversized pieces of cake. He traveled for weeks with friends and family, spending his severance money living a lifestyle he loved.

Between travels we met for coffee one weekend. After hearing of his adventures, I asked him why he was making the choices he was. His answer was from the heart.

"I'd rather die and die happy and not lose my friends and wife than to be miserable without them and be alive."

A few months later he died.

He lived the life that he wanted right up to the end. But it cost him his life.

Mike was surrounded by naysayers. Even when the stakes were high and the path for healing was clearly understood by all and completely achievable.

As you start to live life with fewer chemicals, you will likely encounter naysayers. It might be your friends. It might be your family. It might be your spouse or kids.

In my own experience, I have had all of those categories of people in my life that started out not understanding. Some people were rude and degrading. I've been called a number of names that I don't care to repeat here.

I've been described as a hippie, natural, and radical. What's funny to me is that living life with fewer chemicals is not hippy or radical. It is becoming a norm. It is becoming mainstream society, and a lot of people are moving towards fewer chemicals.

Organic stores (food with no chemicals) are popping up everywhere, and traditional stores are dedicating space to organic food sections.

Public school educators are teaching students about the chemicals in agriculture classes (which also address organic farming), and about chemicals in our food supplies and how these chemicals are affecting young people's health and behavior.

While it's not a radical idea, it IS still an emerging idea. The general public is trying to wrap their minds around it.

Further, even when people understand one piece, they often times don't understand the full picture. For example, maybe a person understands healthy eating or organic eating, but it's not even on their radar that building products in their home are off-gassing chemicals into the air. Or maybe they understand that cleaners can be toxic but they don't know that their clothing could be causing immune systems to be stressed.

What happens as you start to make changes to live a life with fewer chemicals, is that some of the people you're surrounded by can't relate.

They can't relate to what you're doing. They can't share your excitement. They can't quite get past their surprise that this is what's happening in our world.

How do you handle that?

### Create a Team
Create a team of people that believe you. That understand you. That know this is real. They may not believe in every single detail that you do, but they largely are trying to live their lives the same way.

We all, as human beings, want to be understood. We want to be loved. We don't want people to tell us that we're crazy or outcasts or that we're over the top. Because we're not.

It's emotionally and physically exhausting to constantly have to "prove" to the people close to you that you're not crazy or an outcast or over the top. Spending time that way is a drain of one of the most precious resources we have—time.

Instead, spend the majority of your time surrounded by your team that is there to help you, and you them. I'm not saying you should snub people that don't understand or don't care to. I'm saying to spend limited amounts of time trying to educate those people, while spending most of your time and energy focused on your goal of living life with fewer chemicals.

On your team, include a doctor that has a certification in environmental medicine. That's important in helping to continue to understand exactly what's going on and to create a plan that is tailored to you, particularly if you have medical conditions.

If you choose an MD (medical doctor) that is certified in environmental medicine, they could be helpful in considering how the environment could be impacting your health and couple that with western medicine. The result could be an individual health plan that combines the best of both worlds.

The American Academy of Environmental Medicine has a physician locator on their website[171] that is helpful in finding doctors practicing environmental medicine.

Chiropractors, acupuncturists, and yoga and meditation instructors are all examples of people that typically lead healthier lifestyles and may be in tune to the chemicals in our everyday products. Consider adding these folks to your team if you think they're a good fit for you.

You'll also want a friend or two on your team. Ideally they would be interested in living a similar lifestyle as you.

---

[171] https://www.aaemonline.org/#

However, since living life with fewer chemicals is still an emerging idea (so many people don't know there are chemicals in our everyday products), you may not know one or two friends that are on board with the idea. The next best thing is to identify friends that are supportive in general and are excited about your personal journey, even if they don't understand or believe in living life with fewer chemicals.

Lastly, connect with organizations that are PASSIONATE! about living life with fewer chemicals. These organizations may be closer to you than you think. California and the companies located there have been leaders in educating and producing products with fewer chemicals. But you don't have to live on the coast to have these companies (and people!) close by.

Here in Wisconsin, we have organic GOTS certified wool bed manufacturers, organic veggie farms, and organic dairy farms within a few miles of my favorite places to go. I could literally "drop by"—they are that close. These are companies that are well known nationally. It's incredible to me that companies like this are in our local community.

Other examples of passionate companies (some of which have been mentioned already) are:

- Silent Spring Institute
  (https://www.silentspring.org/)
- Environmental Working Group
  (https://www.ewg.org/)
- Safer Chemicals, Healthy Families
  (http://saferchemicals.org/)
- Campaign for Safer Cosmetics
  (http://www.safecosmetics.org/)

- American Academy of Environmental Medicine (https://www.aaemonline.org)
- Sophia Ruan Gushee of Practical Nontoxic Living (https://www.nontoxicliving.tips/)
- Debra Lynn Dadd (http://www.debralynndadd.com/)
- The Minimalists (https://www.theminimalists.com/)
- ...and many, many others.

Become surrounded by people that can help you live life with fewer chemicals, and help them out as well!  Become connected to these types of companies and join their social media communities.

In addition to groups passionate about living life with fewer chemicals, join groups that will help you achieve related goals, such as scaling back on the number of items in your home.

Groups like The Minimalists may be helpful to have on your team if you subscribe to the idea that less is more (thereby reducing the number of chemicals that may be off-gassing in your home). The Minimalist group could help with the "buy less items" side, and others on your team could help with the less chemical portion of your lifestyle change.

So what do you do with your team?

Run ideas past them, get together for tea, send each other helpful tips or information, and have fun with it!

Offer to help people on your team in choosing products that are healthier. And ask them for what you want to know or need help with.

## Ask for What You Want or Need

It's amazing how little we, myself included, actually ask others for what we want or need. We're paralyzed by fear and tell ourselves that so and so doesn't have time for me, or that person would never return my call.

And we never even try.

But when we do, doors start to open.

People love to help other people.

Even if that person can't help you in the moment, they come across people or resources and think of you. This has happened to me many times, but the most memorable moment I have was from 2010.

I was looking to purchase a home built between 1960 and 1975 that had not been updated, and therefore would contain fewer chemicals from new products off-gassing. I explained this in a letter along with a short reason of why. I printed multiple copies of the letter, hand signed every one, and mailed them to over 100 homes in the town I lived in.

Silence. I didn't receive one response.

Fast forward seven years to 2017. One of the letter recipients, Kate, was ready to sell her home and move to a retirement facility. She remembered the letter I had sent back in 2010 and offered to sell her home to me, before it was advertised as being for sale or listed with a realtor.

Had I not asked for what I wanted or needed, I would not have had the opportunity to buy her home.

On a smaller scale, this occurs daily.

People telling other people that they're looking for organic soap, and voila! They think of the place they happened to see an organic soap display.

If you don't put it out there, if you don't ask people for what you want or need, they don't know and they can't help you.

I've had my share of unpleasant experiences in this world, but largely the number of amazing people and amazing opportunities out there for all of us to connect to, far exceed what we think is possible.

You just never know what will happen, if you just ask.

# Resources

## Books

Borges, Marco. *The 22-Day Revolution*. New York: Celebra, a division of Penguin Group, 2015.

Carr, Kris. Crazy Sexy Diet. Connecticut: Globe Pequot Press, 2011.

Gushee, Sophia Ruan. *A to Z of D-Toxing: The Ultimate Guide to Reducing Our Toxic Exposures*. New York: The S File Publishing, LLC, 2015.

## Reports & Studies

Agency for Toxic Substance and Disease Registry (ATSDR), Division of Health Assessment and Consultation. "Health Effects of Chemical Exposure." Accessed February 7, 2017. doi: CS214865-D
https://www.atsdr.cdc.gov/emes/public/docs/Health%20Effects%20of%20Chemical%20Exposure%20FS.pdf

Agency for Toxic Substance and Disease Registry (ATSDR), Division of Health Assessment and Consultation. "Chemicals, Cancer, and You." Accessed December 12, 2015. doi:CS218078A
https://www.atsdr.cdc.gov/emes/public/docs/Chemicals,%20Cancer,%20and%20You%20FS.pdf

Agency for Toxic Substance and Disease Registry (ATSDR). "Module Two, Routes of Exposure." Training Manual. Accessed January 19, 2018.
https://www.atsdr.cdc.gov/training/toxmanual/pdf/module-2.pdf

Breast Cancer Fund. "Disrupted Development: The Dangers of Prenatal BPA Exposure." September 2013.
https://d124kohvtzl951.cloudfront.net/wp-content/uploads/2017/03/02025229/Report_Disrupted-Development-the-Dangers-of-Prenatal-BPA-Exposure_September_2013.pdf

Healthy Building Network. "Toxic Chemicals in Building Materials: An Overview for Health Care Organizations." Fact Sheet: Toxic Chemicals in Building Materials. May 2008.
https://healthybuilding.net/uploads/files/toxic-chemicals-in-building-materials.pdf

National Institute of Health, National Institute of Arthritis and Musculoskeletal and Skin Diseases. "Understanding Autoimmune Diseases." March 2016: 1.
doi: NIH Publication No. 16–7582
https://www.niams.nih.gov/sites/default/files/catalog/files/understanding_autoimmune.pdf

United States Department of Agriculture, Agricultural Marketing Service. National Organic Program. "Cosmetics, Body Care Products, and Personal Care Products." April 2008.
https://www.ams.usda.gov/sites/default/files/media/OrganicCosmeticsFactSheet.pdf

## Articles

Becker, Joshua. "21 Surprising Statistics That Reveal How Much Stuff We Actually Own." becomingminimalist. Accessed March 23, 2017.
https://www.becomingminimalist.com/clutter-stats/

Boyle, Megan, Samara Geller. "Skip the Fabric Softeners." Environmental Working Group. May 5, 2016.
https://www.ewg.org/enviroblog/2016/05/skip-fabric-softeners#.WlmQ0qinHIV

Breast Cancer Fund, Campaign for Safe Cosmetics. "Anti-Aging Secrets Exposed, Chemical Linked to Breast Cancer in Skin Care." October 2015.
http://www.safecosmetics.org/wp-content/uploads/2015/10/Anti-aging-secrets-exposed-report.pdf

Center for Science in the Public Interest. "First-ever Study Reveals Amounts of Food Dyes in Brand-name Foods: Amounts in Some Foods Exceed Levels Used in Many Tests of Dyes' Impact on Children's Behavior." May 7, 2014.
https://cspinet.org/new/201405071.html

DellaValle, Curt. "The Pollution in People: Cancer-Causing Chemicals in Americans' Bodies." EWG Original Research, June 14, 2016. https://www.ewg.org/research/pollution-people#.WllIyqinHIU .

Environmental Working Group. "EWG's Dirty Dozen Guide to Food Additives." November, 12, 2014. https://www.ewg.org/research/ewg-s-dirty-dozen-guide-food-additives?gclid=CjwKEAiAz4XFBRCW87vj6-28uFMSJAAHeGZbgEvzi_SxO4-WHgqQoeObIQULww_ubP-CHplQ_hUyZBoCLPLw_wcB#.Wll-XKinHIU

Formuzls, Alex, Violet Batcha. "IQs Plummet And Healthcare Costs Surge From Endocrine Disrupting Chemicals." Environmental Working Group, October 20, 2016. http://www.ewg.org/enviroblog/2016/10/iqs-plummet-and-healthcare-costs-surge-endocrine-disrupting-chemicals#.WdPu8mhSzIU

GreenPeace, "Hazardous substances reduced but not eliminated from Laptops," Feature Story. October 23, 2007. http://www.greenpeace.org/international/en/news/features/hazardous-substances-laptops/

Healthy Child Healthy World. "4 Nontoxic Cleaners That Should be in Every Home." http://www.healthychild.org/4-nontoxic-cleaners-that-should-be-in-every-home/

HealthyStuff and Campaign for Healthier Solutions. "New Dollar Store Study Released." *EcologyCenter*, February 4, 2015. https://www.ecocenter.org/article/hs-news-news/new-dollar-store-study-released

James, Maia. "Safe Laundry Detergent Guide." Gimme the Good Stuff. January 20, 2013. https://gimmethegoodstuff.org/safe-product-guides/laundry-detergent/

Lee, Professor Tang G. "Vital Signs, Health and the Built Environment: Indoor Air Quality." The University of Calgary. Accessed October 24, 2016 and January 19, 2018. http://www.mtpinnacle.com/pdfs/iaq.pdf

Morrisson, Chris. "How Dryer Sheets Work." How Stuff Works. November 30, 2009.
https://home. howstuffworks.com/dryer-sheets2.htm

Physicians for Social Responsibility. "Toxic Chemicals in our Food System." Fact Sheet, Accessed February 13, 2017: 1.
http://www.psr.org/assets/pdfs/toxic-chemicals-in-our-food.pdf

Rudel, A. Ruthann, et all. New Exposure Biomarkers as Tools for Breast Cancer Epidemiology, Biomonitoring, and Prevention: A Systematic Approach Based on Animal Evidence. Environmental Health Perspectives.
doi: 10.1289/ehp.1307455
https://ehp.niehs.nih.gov/1307455/

Scranton, Alex. "Ditch the Dryer Sheets!" Women's Voices for the Earth. April 4, 2013.
https://www.womensvoices.org/2013/04/04/ditch-the-dryer-sheets/

Sennebogen, Emily. "Do clothes always shrink if you wash in warm water?" How Stuff Works. April 13, 2012.
https://home.howstuffworks.com/home-improvement/household-hints-tips/cleaning-organizing/do-clothes-always-shrink-if-you-wash-in-warm-water.htm

Stolber, Tasha, Jamee Hood. "How to Remove Toxic Dust, Your Home's Most Unwanted Guest." EWG News and Analysis. Environmental Working Group, November 9, 2017.
https://www.ewg.org/enviroblog/2017/11/how-remove-toxic-dust-your-home-s-most-unwanted-guest#.Wlzcj6inHIU

Sutton, Rebecca. "Don't get slimed: Skip the fabric softener." Environmental Working Group. News and Analysis. November 1, 2011.
https://www.ewg.org/enviroblog/2011/11/dont-get-slimed-skip-fabric-softener#.WlmSe6inHIV

U.S. Department of Agriculture, USDA National Organic Program. "Labeling Organic Products." December 2016.
https://www.ams.usda.gov/sites/default/files/media/Labeling%20Organic%20Products.pdf

U.S. Environmental Protection Agency. "The Inside Story: A Guide to Indoor Air Quality." Indoor Air Quality. Accessed February 27, 2017. https://www.epa.gov/indoor-air-quality-iaq/inside-story-guide-indoor-air-quality

Warhurst, Michael. "It's a No Brainer! Action needed to stop children being exposed to chemicals that harm their brain development!" March 7, 2017.
http://www.chemtrust.org/brain/

Young, Saundra. "Endangering the Next Generation of Brains." Our Toxic Times. Chemical Injury Information Network, March 2014, Volume 25, Number 3: 2-3.

## **Websites**

Agency for Toxic Substance & Disease Registry (ASTDR). "Why Are Children Often Especially Susceptible to the Adverse Effects of Environmental Toxicants?" Principles of Pediatric Environmental Health. February 15, 2016.
https://www.atsdr.cdc.gov/csem/csem.asp?csem=27&po=3

Agricultural Marketing Resource Center. "Cotton." Profile revised September 2017.
https://www.agmrc.org/commodities-products/fiber/cotton/

American Cancer Society. "Teflon and Perfluorooctanoic Acid (PFOA), What are Teflon and PFOA? Where are they found?" What Causes Cancer. Last Revised January 5, 2016.
https://www.cancer.org/cancer/cancer-causes/teflon-and-perfluorooctanoic-acid-pfoa.html

American Chemical. "Textile Chemistry." Overview, Accessed November 23, 2017.
https://www.acs.org/content/acs/en/careers/college-to-career/chemistry-careers/textile-chemistry.html

American Skin Association. "Healthy Skin." Date Accessed, March 7, 2017.
http://www.americanskin.org/resource/

Autism Speaks. "Deeper Understanding of Link between Chemical Pollutants and Autism." Accessed January 19, 2018. https://www.autismspeaks.org/science/science-news/top-ten-lists/2012/deeper-understanding-link-chemical-pollutants-and-autism

Berkley Lab. "Indoor Air Quality." Scientific Findings Resource Bank. Accessed January 12, 2018. https://iaqscience.lbl.gov/voc-svocs

Borrell, Brendan. "Where does blue food dye come from?" Scientific American. January 2009. https://www.scientificamerican.com/article/where-does-blue-food-dye/

BreastCancer.org. "Exposure to Chemicals in Food." Accessed February 9, 2017. http://www.breastcancer.org/risk/factors/food_chem

BreastCancer.org. "U.S. Breast Cancer Statistics." Last Modified January 9, 2018. http://www.breastcancer.org/symptoms/understand_bc/statistics

Centers for Disease Control and Prevention. "Expected New Cancer Cases and Deaths in 2020." Page last reviewed: June 24, 2015. https://www.cdc.gov/cancer/dcpc/research/articles/cancer_2020.htm

Chemical Injury.net. "About Dr. Grace Ziem." Accessed February 7, 2017. http://www.chemicalinjury.net/biosketch.htm

Chemical Injury.net. "How Chemical Injury/Chemical Sensitivity Affects the Body." Accessed February 7, 2017. http://chemicalinjury.net/html/how_chemical_injury_chemical_s.html

Chemical Injury.net. "How Chemical Injury/Chemical Sensitivity Affects the Body (pg 2)." Accessed February 7, 2017. http://www.chemicalinjury.net/html/how_chemical_injury_chemical_s1.html

Chemical Injury.net. "Long Term Treatment (pg11)." Accessed February 7, 2017. http://www.chemicalinjury.net/html/neural_sensitization-pg_11.html

Chemical Injury.net. "Neutral Sensitization: The Medical Key to Treatment of Chemical Injury." Accessed February 7, 2017. http://www.chemicalinjury.net/html/neural_sensitization__the_medi.html

Chemical Injury.net. "Neutral Sensitization: The Medical Key to Treatment of Chemical Injury (pg2)." Accessed February 7, 2017. http://www.chemicalinjury.net/html/neural_sensitization-pg_2.html

Chemical Injury.net. "Preventing Chemical Injury." Accessed February 8, 2017. http://www.chemicalinjury.net/preventingchemicalinjury.htm

City of Phoenix. "Flammable Fabrics." Accessed November 23, 2017. https://www.phoenix.gov/fire/safety-information/home/fabrics

Coyuchi. "Why use low-impact dyes?" August 8, 2017. https://www.coyuchi.com/the-naturalista/lowimpactdyes/

Debra Lynn Dadd. "About Debra Lynn Dadd." Accessed October 17, 2017. http://www.debralynndadd.com/about-debra/

Debra Lynn Dadd. "Stainless Steel Leaching Into Food and Beverages." Q & A, January 17, 2010. http://www.debralynndadd.com/q-a/stainless-steel-leaching-into-food-and-beverages/

Dictionary.com, "Synthetic." http://www.dictionary.com/browse/synthetic?s=t

Ecology Center, "Adverse Health Effects of Plastics," Accessed November 20, 2017. https://ecologycenter.org/factsheets/adverse-health-effects-of-plastics/

Environmental Health Center – Dallas. "Chemicals and You." Accessed January 19, 2018. https://www.ehcd.com/chemicals-and-you/

Environmental Working Group. "EWG's Dirty Dozen: Cancer Prevention Edition." Rethink Cancer, Accessed January 15, 2018. https://www.ewg.org/cancer/EWGs-dirty-dozen-cancer-prevention-edition.php#.WlzhGqinHIV

Environmental Working Group. "Executive Summary: EWG's 2017 Shopper's Guide to Pesticides in Produce." Accessed January 12, 2018. https://www.ewg.org/foodnews/summary.php#.Wlzv9KinHIU

Environmental Working Group. "'Yoga Mat' Chemicals Found in nearly 500 Foods." Updated February 28, 2014. https://www.ewg.org/release/yoga-mat-chemical-found-nearly-500-foods#.Wll8h6inHIU

Environmental Working Group and the Campaign for Safe Cosmetics. "Hidden Chemicals in Perfume and Cologne." Not So Sexy. May 12, 2010.

Formuzis, Alex and Violet Batcha. "IQs Plummet and Healthcare Costs Surge From Endocrine Disrupting Chemicals." EWG News and Analysis. October 20, 2016. https://www.ewg.org/enviroblog/2016/10/iqs-plummet-and-healthcare-costs-surge-endocrine-disrupting-chemicals#.WlldJKinHIU

Global Organic Textile Standard. "General Description." Ecology & Social Responsibility. Last Updated May 23, 2017. http://www.global-standard.org/the-standard.html

Global Organic Textile Standard. "The Standard." Ecology & Social Responsibility. Last Updated May 23, 2017. http://www.global-standard.org/the-standard.html

Green America. "Green Dry Cleaning." Accessed February 27, 2017. https://www.greenamerica.org/green-living/green-dry-cleaning

Halvorson, Christine. "Uses for Vinegar: Doing Laundry." https://home.howstuffworks.com/home-improvement/household-hints-tips/cleaning-organizing/uses-for-vinegar-doing-laundry-ga.htm

HealthyStuff. "Chemical hazards found in kitchen, exercise equipment, jewelry, consumer electronics, building and outdoor products. Some retailers responding, others remain silent. " Fall 2013 Product Survey Results Released, November 15, 2013. https://www.ecocenter.org/healthy-stuff/reports/fall-2013-product-survey-results-released

Kids Health. "Your Immune System." Date Reviewed: May 2015.

http://kidshealth.org/en/kids/immune.html?ref=search#

Lowimpact.org. "Natural dyes: Introduction."
https://www.lowimpact.org/lowimpact-topic/natural-dyes/

Minnesota Department of Health. "Chemicals of Special Concern to Children's Health," Children's Environmental Health. Accessed January 19, 2018.
http://www.health.state.mn.us/divs/eh/children/chemicals.html

National Institute of Environmental Health Sciences. "Neurological Diseases and Disorders" Climate and Human Health. Last Reviewed July 20, 2017.
https://www.niehs.nih.gov/research/programs/geh/climatechange/heal th_impacts/neurological_diseases/index.cfm

National Institute of Health, Eunice Kennedy Shriver National Institute of Child Health and Human Development. "What are the parts of the nervous system?" Health research throughout the lifespan. Accessed February 27, 2017.
https://www.nichd.nih.gov/health/topics/neuro/conditioninfo/parts

National Institute of Health, National Cancer Institute. "Introduction to the Endocrine." SEER Training Module. Accessed February 22, 2017.
https://training.seer.cancer.gov/anatomy/endocrine/

National Institute of Health, National Cancer Institute. "Introduction to the Lymphatic System." SEER Training Module. Accessed February 22, 2017.
https://training.seer.cancer.gov/anatomy/lymphatic/

National Institute of Health, National Cancer Institute. "Introduction to the Nervous System." SEER Training Module. Accessed February 22, 2017.
https://training.seer.cancer.gov/anatomy/nervous/

National Institute of Health, National Cancer Institute. "Introduction to the Reproductive System." SEER Training Module. Accessed February 22, 2017.
https://training.seer.cancer.gov/anatomy/reproductive/

National Institute of Health, National Cancer Institute. "Introduction to the Respiratory System." SEER Training Module. Accessed February 22, 2017.
https://training.seer.cancer.gov/anatomy/respiratory/

National Institute of Health, National Cancer Institute. "Introduction to the Urinary System." SEER Training Module. Accessed February 22, 2017.
https://training.seer.cancer.gov/anatomy/urinary/

National Institute of Health, National Institute of Allergy and Infectious Diseases. "Autoimmune Diseases." Accessed March 9, 2017.
https://www.niaid.nih.gov/diseases-conditions/autoimmune-diseases

National Institute of Neurological Disorders and Stroke. "Brain Basics; Understanding Sleep."
https://www.ninds.nih.gov/Disorders/Patient-Caregiver-Education/Understanding-Sleep

Nolte, Kurt. "Pima cotton," Yuma County Cooperative Extension.
https://cals.arizona.edu/fps/sites/cals.arizona.edu.fps/files/cotw/Pima_Cotton.pdf

Office on Women's Health, U.S. Department of Health and Human Services. "What's happening during the typical 28-day menstrual cycle?" Page last updated October 16, 2017.
https://www.womenshealth.gov/menstrual-cycle/your-menstrual-cycle#3

Organic Lifestyle. "Fiber Reactive / Low Impact dyes."
https://organiclifestyle.com/articles/fibre-reactive-low-impact-dyes?currency_code=USD

Petroleum Services Association of Canada. "Clothing." Facts about Canada's Oil and Natural Gas Industry. Accessed March 26, 2017.
https://oilandgasinfo.ca/products/clothing/

Prevent Cancer Foundation. "Reduce Cancer Risk." Accessed March 23, 2017.
https://preventcancer.org/learn/

Public Broadcasting Station. "PBS KIDS Partners with Whole Foods Market to Launch New Sustainable, Non-Toxic Toys This Holiday Season." Press Releases, November 5, 2015. http://www.pbs.org/about/blogs/news/pbs-kids-partners-with-whole-foods-market-to-launch-new-sustainable-non-toxic-toys-this-holiday-season/

Rodale Institute. "Chemical cotton." Dig Deeper. February 4, 2014. https://rodaleinstitute.org/chemical-cotton/

Science Buddies. "Staining Science: Make the Boldest, Brightest Dye!" A colorful challenge from Science Buddies. Scientific American. January 2009. https://www.scientificamerican.com/article/bring-science-home-brightest-dye/

Sustainable Design Award. Kate Fletcher. "Natural Textiles." 1999. http://www.sda-uk.org/materials/textiles/natural_textiles.htm

The Essential Chemical Industry – online, "Colorants," Date last amended March 18, 2013. http://essentialchemicalindustry.org/materials-and-applications/colorants.html

The Food Revolution Network. "10 Banned Foods Americans Should Stop Eating." October 2, 2014. https://foodrevolution.org/blog/10-banned-foods-americans-stop-eating/

The Synthetic & Rayon Textiles Export Promotion Council, "About Us," Accessed March 23, 2017. http://www.synthetictextiles.org/

U.S. Department of Labor, Bureau of Labor Statistics. "How Much Do Consumers Spend on Apparel?" Spotlight on Statistics. https://www.bls.gov/spotlight/2012/fashion/

U.S. Environmental Protection Agency. "Introduction to Indoor Air Quality." Last Updated January 26, 2017. https://www.epa.gov/indoor-air-quality-iaq/introduction-indoor-air-quality

U.S. Food & Drug Administration. "Small Businesses & Homemade Cosmetics: Fact Sheet." Cosmetics. Accessed January 19, 2018. https://www.fda.gov/cosmetics/resourcesforyou/industry/ucm388736.htm#7

U.S. Patent and Trademark Office. "Trade Secret Policy." May 11, 2016. https://www.uspto.gov/patents-getting-started/international-protection/trade-secret-policy

University at Buffalo, The State University of New York. "How Chemicals Enter the Body." Accessed March 23, 2017. https://www.buffalo.edu/facilities/ehs/training/right-to-know-training/how-chemicals-enter-the-body.html

World Health Organization. "Cancer." Fact sheet. February 2017. http://www.who.int/mediacentre/factsheets/fs297/en/

## Video

The C Word Movie. *Think Big Tobacco Is Bad? Look at Big Food.* Video. Directed by Meghan L. O'Hara. Performed by Morgan Freeman. 2016. Zorro and Me Films Production. Accessed on Robyn O'Brien "Morgan Freeman Shows Us How Big Tobacco Became Big Food." February 1, 2017. https://robynobrien.com/morgan-freeman-shows-us-how-big-tobacco-became-big-food/

National Geographic. *Human Body 10.* Video. Accessed February 7, 2017. https://www.nationalgeographic.com/science/health-and-human-body/human-body/

Public Broadcasting Station. *How You Should Be Doing Laundry.* Performed by Randy and Jason. Aired 12/31/15. Public Broadcasting Station. 2015.

# ABOUT THE AUTHOR

Angela Cummings is a writer, consultant and wellness champion, with a passion for helping others live an organic chemical-free lifestyle.

Since 2014, Angela has been a professional freelance writer and consultant. She has educated common Joes, construction contractors, and organic eaters about the chemicals found in everyday products. In particular, she has taught others how to choose food, clothing, personal care items, household products and building materials (and design and processes) that can lead to a healthier home with the least amount of chemicals possible.

Angela has been a contributing author for Practical Nontoxic Living (http://www.nontoxicliving.tips), and ghost writer of healthy marketing materials for companies located in Southeastern Wisconsin. Recently, she became a contributing author for The Mighty (https://themighty.com), a website dedicated to empowering and connecting people with health conditions and disabilities.

Her company, Occupant Wellness, has provided consulting and education to people looking to live a healthier lifestyle with fewer chemicals. Angela has utilized her Bachelor's Degree in Management and Associates Degree in Marketing to shape her consulting and educational services in a way that resonates with people.

Angela lives in Sussex, Wisconsin and provides writing and consulting services throughout the U.S.

For more information about Occupant Wellness services go to: https://www.occupantwellness.com/.

Contact Angela directly at occupantwellness@gmail.com.

Made in the USA
Lexington, KY
25 March 2019